Getting Started with ownCloud

The only precise guide to help you set up and scale
ownCloud for personal and commercial usage

Aditya Patawari

[PACKT] open source*
PUBLISHING   community experience distilled

BIRMINGHAM - MUMBAI

Getting Started with ownCloud

First published: July 2013

Production Reference: 1170713

Published by Packt Publishing Ltd.
Livery Place
35 Livery Street
Birmingham B3 2PB, UK.

ISBN 978-1-78216-825-6

www.packtpub.com

Cover Image by Abhishek Pandey (abhishek.pandey1210@gmail.com)

Credits

Author
Aditya Patawari

Reviewers
Frank Karlitschek
ADEOTI Olusola Adekunle
Jos Poortvliet

Acquisition Editor
Rebecca Youe

Commissioning Editor
Harsha Bharwani

Technical Editors
Ruchita Bhansali
Shashank Desai
Krishnaveni Haridas

Project Coordinator
Romal Karani

Proofreader
Clyde Jenkins

Indexer
Rekha Nair

Production Coordinator
Arvindkumar Gupta

Cover Work
Arvindkumar Gupta

Foreword

There are many advantages of storing data in the cloud such as ubiquitous access to data from multiple devices, social interaction, sharing with others on the web, and no extra software to install. However, in exchange for this privilege, your data is often stored on, and owned by one of several organizations, none of which easily allow interaction or sharing of data among them. Besides these convenience issues, there are also problems with privacy and security, because the potential of one hardware failure makes the data of thousands of users impossible to access. Taken together, the cloud is not perfect.

ownCloud is the first and most ubiquitous FOSS solution to run on the server or computer of the user, or on an internal company server giving the user the benefits of cloud computing and control of the data. ownCloud integrates with desktop applications, so that the users have cloud features combined with the security and the good cost structure of in-house file servers.

This was my main motivation for starting the ownCloud free software project in 2010 and also ownCloud Inc. later. Aditya is an active member of the ownCloud community for a long time, and I'm happy that he collected a lot of useful information for beginners and advanced users here in this book. Have fun reading it.

Frank Karlitschek
Founder of ownCloud

About the Author

Aditya Patawari is a Systems Engineer by profession, and just loves to play around with Linux. He works on various parts of system lifecycles, and handles infrastructure automation and scaling of applications. He is also a contributor at Fedora project, and can be heard talking about the same along with the Linux systems automation at several conferences and events. His first contact with ownCloud was a year ago when he was just a student, and ownCloud itself was less than a year old, and a part of KDE project.

This book would have been very difficult to write without the support of my family, my parents and my brother, Nishchay. I would like to thank all my friends too for believing in me even when I was full of doubts and for bringing me down to earth when I was too much of me. A humble thanks and appreciation to Frank Karlitschek, founder of ownCloud, and entire ownCloud community for the support I have received throughout the writing of the book. A huge thank you to the entire Packt Publishing team, which made the process much smoother and easier for me.

About the Reviewers

Frank Karlitschek is a long-time open source contributor and former board member of the KDE e.V. He managed engineering teams for over 10 years, and worked as head of a unit, and managing director at different Internet companies. Since 2007, he is heading a startup which develops social networking and e-commerce products for several fortune 500 companies. In 2010, he started the ownCloud project and is leading the community project since then. In 2011, he founded ownCloud Inc. together with Markus Rex and Holger Dyroff from SUSE to offer commercial services around ownCloud.

> I want to thank the ownCloud open source community for helping me to build and shape this great piece of software. ownCloud only exists today because of over 100 volunteered contributors. Thanks a lot to everyone.

ADEOTI Olusola Adekunle is studying computer science and engineering at Crown Polytechnic, Ado Ekiti, and Nigeria. He has experience in web development and maintenance.

He is the CEO of ADAD Technologies, the owners of www.onthirdplanetsms.com, which is a bulk SMS website, and the owner of www.onthirdplanet.com, that is a tech blog. He has also worked on the Monetizing Your Hobbies book.

I will like to appreciate all my friends, family, staffs of ADAD Technologies, and most especially my parents – Mr. and Mrs. ADEOTI Gbenga for their support both financially and morally.

My appreciation also goes to Packt Publishing for giving me the opportunity of reviewing this book.

Thank you all and God bless.

Jos Poortvliet has been a Free Software evangelist for over 10 years, and had been involved in a variety of communities. He has been active as marketing team lead in the KDE community, coordinating marketing activities, and taking care of press and promo for the cross-project Gran Canaria and Berlin Desktop Summits, and several academy conferences. He currently works for SUSE Linux as community manager, handling communication around the openSUSE community, and taking care of merchandising and event management.

You can find out what he's up to at his blog on jospoortvliet.com.

www.PacktPub.com

Support files, eBooks, discount offers and more

You might want to visit www.PacktPub.com for support files and downloads related to your book.

Did you know that Packt offers eBook versions of every book published, with PDF and ePub files available? You can upgrade to the eBook version at www.PacktPub.com and as a print book customer, you are entitled to a discount on the eBook copy. Get in touch with us at service@packtpub.com for more details.

At www.PacktPub.com, you can also read a collection of free technical articles, sign up for a range of free newsletters and receive exclusive discounts and offers on Packt books and eBooks.

http://PacktLib.PacktPub.com

Do you need instant solutions to your IT questions? PacktLib is Packt's online digital book library. Here, you can access, read, and search across Packt's entire library of books.

Why Subscribe?

- Fully searchable across every book published by Packt
- Copy and paste, print and bookmark content
- On demand and accessible via web browser

Free Access for Packt account holders

If you have an account with Packt at www.PacktPub.com, you can use this to access PacktLib today and view nine entirely free books. Simply use your login credentials for immediate access.

Table of Contents

Preface

The primary objective of this book is to provide an introduction to ownCloud, the different scenarios and use cases for it. It'll help beginners and new users to do a basic setup and use ownCloud in their daily lives. The book will also be helpful for advanced users and system administrators who want to indulge in slightly complex tasks such as LDAP integration and backups. For app developers, the book contains an introduction on developing ownCloud apps. After reading this book, the reader should be able to manage personal as well as corporate instances of ownCloud easily.

ownCloud's benefits are manifolds. While many reader might think of it as a tool to store and share files, it is much more than that. In today's world, protecting one's data and privacy from malicious elements on the Internet is of utmost importance. ownCloud gives the user control to their data. Encryption further strengthens the data confidentiality. With ownCloud apps, the functionality of ownCloud increases to a level where it has no match.

What this book covers

Chapter 1, Setting up ownCloud will get the reader started with ownCloud installation. It covers steps to install ownCloud on different operating systems. It also gives minor tweaks for improving the usability and helps the reader in picking up the right database for the different scenarios they may face.

Chapter 2, Usage of ownCloud and Its Apps introduces the reader to some common uses and apps of ownCloud. The chapter shows how common tasks such as uploading and sharing files can be done with ease using ownCloud. ownCloud's syncing capabilities among multitude of devices is highlighted here. Reader will also get a grasp of how to manage events and appointments using the ownCloud Calendar app, and how to use the ownCloud contacts app to maintain address books. We take a step ahead and talk about how to sync the Calendar events and contacts to a compatible third-party application.

Chapter 3, User Management And Admin Tools starts with introducing readers to basic administrative tasks such as users and group creation and management. It goes ahead deeper to accommodate corporate administrators who want to integrate LDAP or Active Directory with ownCloud. Later in the chapter, tips about how to enable file versioning and ZIP downloads are provided.

Chapter 4, Securing your ownCloud will help the readers in increasing the security of their web servers, Apache and Microsoft IIS. Further, the way to secure ownCloud data directory is discussed. Some standard MySQL securing tips are also provided in this chapter. At the end, there is an introductory text to ownCloud encryption.

Chapter 5, ownCloud Backup, Restore, and Logging discusses some common methods of backing up ownCloud and various other components such as database and restoring an ownCloud instance from the backups created before. Readers will also get to know about setting up a syslog server and configuring it to receive ownCloud logs.

Chapter 6, Load Balancing and HA for ownCloud provides with some basic strategies for load balancing large scale ownCloud installations. Readers will learn about setting up shared storage systems, for example, WebDAV and using them for storage instead of regular filesystem. Various load balancing algorithms and methods for Apache and Microsoft IIS are also discussed. At the end, we'll see how to use MySQL cluster feature to scale MySQL database as well.

Chapter 7, ownCloud Application Development will introduce the readers to ownCloud application development. This is particularly helpful to those who wish to extend the functionality of ownCloud. This chapter also presents a walk through a pre-written app as an example to make understand much easier.

What you need for this book

The following are the minimum requirements for setting up ownCloud:

- A web server (Apache or IIS)
- PHP and certain PHP libraries as discussed in *Chapter 1, Setting up ownCloud*
- A database (MySQL or SQLite)

Other than these requirements, a reader may install certain other components as per the interest and requirement. These tools and software are discussed in chapters individually.

Who this book is for

This book is for all the ownCloud enthusiasts as well as ownCloud professionals. It'll help users in setting up and maintaining ownCloud instances easily while introducing them to the intricacies of the various setups.

Conventions

In this book, you will find a number of styles of text that distinguish between different kinds of information. Here are some examples of these styles, and an explanation of their meaning.

Code words in text are shown as follows: "JavaScript files goes in the `js` directory."

A block of code is set as follows:

```
<Location />
          DAV On
          AuthType Basic
          AuthName "webdav"
          AuthUserFile /var/www/webdav/passwd.dav
          Require valid-user
</Location>
</VirtualHost>
```

Any command-line input or output is written as follows:

```
sudo yum install cadaver

cadaverhttp://webdav.owncloudbook.com
```

New terms and **important words** are shown in bold. Words that you see on the screen, in menus or dialog boxes for example, appear in the text like this: "We will first have to go to the **Familiar Apps** section."

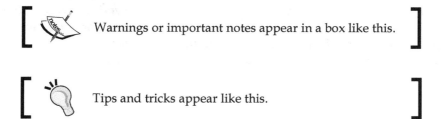

Warnings or important notes appear in a box like this.

Tips and tricks appear like this.

Reader feedback

Feedback from our readers is always welcome. Let us know what you think about this book — what you liked or may have disliked. Reader feedback is important for us to develop titles that you really get the most out of.

To send us general feedback, simply send an e-mail to feedback@packtpub.com, and mention the book title via the subject of your message.

If there is a topic that you have expertise in and you are interested in either writing or contributing to a book, see our author guide on www.packtpub.com/authors.

Customer support

Now that you are the proud owner of a Packt book, we have a number of things to help you to get the most from your purchase.

Downloading the example code

You can download the example code files for all Packt books you have purchased from your account at http://www.packtpub.com. If you purchased this book elsewhere, you can visit http://www.packtpub.com/support and register to have the files e-mailed directly to you.

Errata

Although we have taken every care to ensure the accuracy of our content, mistakes do happen. If you find a mistake in one of our books — maybe a mistake in the text or the code — we would be grateful if you would report this to us. By doing so, you can save other readers from frustration and help us improve subsequent versions of this book. If you find any errata, please report them by visiting http://www.packtpub.com/submit-errata, selecting your book, clicking on the **errata submission form** link, and entering the details of your errata. Once your errata are verified, your submission will be accepted and the errata will be uploaded on our website, or added to any list of existing errata, under the Errata section of that title. Any existing errata can be viewed by selecting your title from http://www.packtpub.com/support.

Piracy

Piracy of copyright material on the Internet is an ongoing problem across all media. At Packt, we take the protection of our copyright and licenses very seriously. If you come across any illegal copies of our works, in any form, on the Internet, please provide us with the location address or website name immediately so that we can pursue a remedy.

Please contact us at copyright@packtpub.com with a link to the suspected pirated material.

We appreciate your help in protecting our authors, and our ability to bring you valuable content.

Questions

You can contact us at questions@packtpub.com if you are having a problem with any aspect of the book, and we will do our best to address it.

1
Setting up ownCloud

Setting up ownCloud is not a very difficult task, especially on Linux, where building a LAMP stack is quite easy. ownCloud can be installed in less than 10 minutes for a small number of users. Being a web application, most of the components can be easily scaled to support thousands of users seamlessly. We are going to talk about some basic installation methods in this chapter, and then look into the scaling aspects in the subsequent chapters.

Installing ownCloud on Linux

There is more than one way to install ownCloud on Linux, depending upon the Linux distribution you run. We'll talk about two major Linux distributions, namely, Fedora and Ubuntu, but we can always find the most up to date, installable packages for various distributions at `http://software.opensuse.org/package/owncloud`. These packages are built and maintained by the people behind ownCloud themselves.

Fedora

Let's do a source install in Fedora. First, we need to install all the dependencies for ownCloud. This includes a web server of our choice, and certain PHP dependencies. For the sake of this demo, we'll use Apache web server and PHP5.

```
yum install -y httpd php php-gd php-mbstring php-pdo php-dom
```

Let us see the use of each of these requirements:

- php-gd: It is used to create and manipulate image files. It can also direct image streams to the browser.

- php-mbstring: It handles multibyte string functions. Several languages have characters which are not representable using one-to-one mapping to a single byte (8 bits). php-mbstring handles character encoding conversion in these cases.

- php-pdo: It provides an interface to communicate with the databases. It very light-weight, and enables database drivers to expose database specific features easily.

- php-dom: It is required to work with XML documents using the DOM API.

Once we have installed the dependencies, download the latest release of ownCloud source from the following link:

http://owncloud.org/install/.

This would be a bzip archive. Extract this to /var/www/html/, and set the owner as Apache user.

```
wget http://download.owncloud.org/community/owncloud-5.0.7.tar.bz2
tar xjvf owncloud-5.0.7.tar.bz2 -C /var/www/html
chown -R /var/www/html/owncloud
```

If security is not a major concern, or if we have other means of securing our server, then we can stop SELinux, otherwise the Apache will keep on throwing an error with 401 return codes, or will complain that the ownCloud directory is not writable.

```
setenforce 0
```

In case disabling the SELinux is not an option, we have to add the files in the ownCloud directory to appropriate SELinux context. We can use chcon to add the entire directory recursively to read-write (rw) context.

```
chcon -R -t httpd_sys_rw_content_t /var/www/html/owncloud
```

Now, we will just open the browser on this computer and go to `http://localhost/ owncloud`. A window will appear similar to the following screenshot:

ownCloud Setup Interface

We need to create the first admin user on this screen. So, fill in a username and a strong password, and click on the **Finish setup** button. We'll take care of the security warning being displayed later in this book. We can try to upload a small file to check. Upload of bigger files will fail at this point of time because of a limit in place by PHP.

Ubuntu

You can use apt manager on Ubuntu and install ownCloud, but first install the dependencies for ownCloud. We'll need Apache web server, PHP, and some other libraries for it to function properly:

```
apt-get install apache2 php5 php5-json php-xml php-mbstring php5-zip curl
apt-get install php5-gd php5-sqlite libcurl3 libcurl3-dev php5-curl php-pdo
apt-get install owncloud
```

The previous command will install ownCloud on our computer.

Installing ownCloud on Windows Server 2008

Let us install ownCloud on a Windows Server 2008. The steps for other Windows versions would be similar. We'll need a web server for it, and **Internet Information Services (IIS)** is a natural choice when it comes to Windows. We also need to have PHP, since ownCloud will not work without it. Installing a database is optional, so we will not get into it right now.

Installing Internet Information Services (IIS)

The following are the steps to install IIS:

1. Go to **Start** menu, and click on **Control Panel**. Select **Programs and Features** and click on **Turn Windows features on or off**.

2. The **Server Manager** will appear. We need to click on **Roles**, and then select **Web Server (IIS)** role. We need to turn on a few features here. Usually the defaults are good enough, but here is a check-list for reference:

   - **Static Content**
   - **Default Document**
   - **Directory Browsing**
   - **HTTP Errors**
   - **CGI**
   - **HTTP Logging**
   - **Request Monitor**
   - **Request Filtering**
   - **Static Content Compression**
   - **IIS Management Console**
   - **IIS Manager Console**

3. Now we need to go to the **Start** menu and click on **IIS Manager**. From here, we can restart the IIS web server.

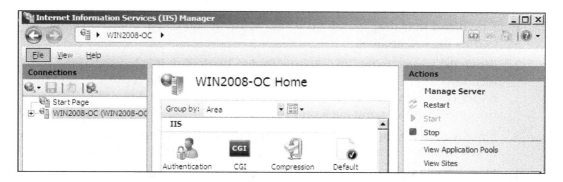

4. Open the browser and go to `http://localhost`. The splash screen for IIS will be displayed.

Installing PHP

Installing PHP for IIS is very straightforward. We just need to download the latest installer from `http://windows.php.net/download/` and run it. At the time of writing this book, PHP 5.3 VC9 x86 was the latest installer available. Select the **IIS FastCGI** radio button when prompted, and install keeping the rest as default.

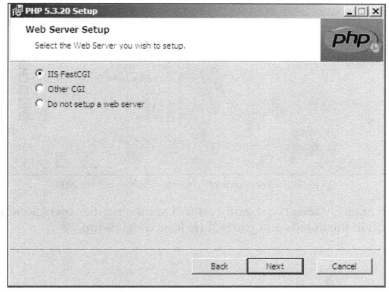

PHP Setup

Installing ownCloud

The following are the steps to install ownCloud on your machine:

1. Download the latest source from `http://owncloud.org/install/` and extract the bz2 archive.

2. Move the source to the IIS `wwwroot` folder. By default it is located at the location `C:\inetpub\wwwroot`. Now we need to give the write access to the folder containing the ownCloud source. To do so we need to right click on the `wwwroot` folder and click on **Properties**.

3. Now from the **security** tab, click on the **Edit** button. Select **Users** from **Group or usernames** list, and then click on the checkbox next to the **Write** option.

4. Now we just need to click on **Apply**, and we are all done.

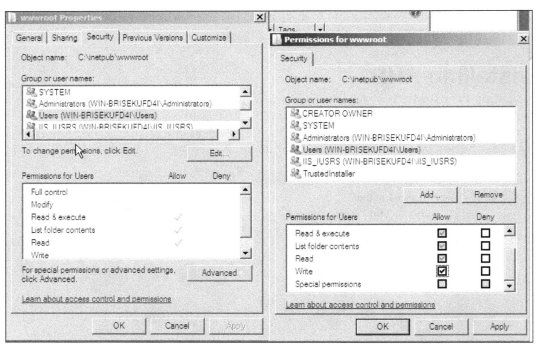

Giving Write Permissions to Users in Windows Server 2008

5. Open `http://localhost` and you will see the regular ownCloud setup page. Just fill in the details and use SQLite for a quick setup.

Giving ownCloud a friendly URL

Now that we have setup our ownCloud instance, we should give it a friendly and short URL for access. This can be done by using virtual hosts' configuration. Virtual host is a web server configuration with which we can give it a name of our choice, provided that we own the domain, and do not reveal the real name of the server. Ideally, we would want to put it under a hostname like http://example.com instead of http://example.com/some-directory/owncloud. The http://example.com is easy to remember and will get the work done faster. If your DNS provider allows, you can even have http://owncloud.example.com to make it more intuitive and relevant. For this, we need to do appropriate virtual host configuration for the web server. So now we get into the Apache config directory and create the vhost.conf file:

```
# cat owncloud-vhost
NameVirtualHost *:80
<VirtualHost *:80>
  ServerAdmin aditya@example.com
  DocumentRoot "/var/www/owncloud/"
  ServerName owncloud.example.com
  ServerAlias owncloud.example.com
  ErrorLog "logs/owncloud/error_log"
  CustomLog "logs/owncloud/access_log"
</VirtualHost>
```

Once the virtual host setup is done, we need to restart the Apache web server. Now we will open our browser and go to http://owncloud.example.com, and we'll see that ownCloud interface opens in this URL.

Coping with large data sets and other PHP fixes

If we try to upload larger files, it will fail. PHP, by default, doesn't allow uploads beyond 2M. This value is defined in the php.ini file. The location of this file varies depending upon the operating system you are using. For Ubuntu, it will be /etc/php5/apache2/php.ini, while for Fedora it is /etc/php.ini. We can always use find command to locate php.ini on our computer.

```
find / -name php.ini
```

We need to find the variable `upload_max_filesize` and `post_max_size`, and increase the limit to a desired value. Ideally, these values should be almost same, with `post_max_size` being slightly higher than `upload_max_filesize`, because there is header information in the posted files. Also if we see a lot of execution time outs, then we should increase `max_execution_time` and `max_input_time` to an appropriate value.

MySQL versus SQLite usage

The choice between MySQL and SQLite depends upon the scale of our deployment. We need to have an estimate of how many users are going to use the instance. For personal deployments with about 15 to 20 users, using SQLite is recommended, because it is easy to install and is inaccessible over the network. It is very lightweight and fast, because there is much less overhead in the terms of connectivity and database driver calls. Usually, the entire database is just a small file of less than 1 MB. If the idea is to deploy ownCloud for a larger scale, like for a large organization or an educational institute, MySQL should be used. MySQL is more scalable, and comes with a lot of features suitable for an enterprise. We can isolate MySQL entirely from the server running ownCloud, reducing load on the server. It is also possible to create MySQL replication and clusters which ensures high-availability and load-balancing of the database. It is also possible to use PostgreSQL which has similar benefits as MySQL. Choosing between MySQL and PostgreSQL is a matter of taste. We will use MySQL for a demo in this book.

Setting up ownCloud with MySQL

Setting up ownCloud with MySQL is very easy. First we need to install MySQL server and `php-mysql` libraries.

- For Ubuntu:

  ```
  apt-get install mysql-server php5-mysql
  ```

- For Fedora:

  ```
  yum install mysql-server php-mysql
  ```

We can enter the root password if the setup prompts for one or we can use `mysqladmin` tool to setup the root password. Now, we need to create the database and the user for ownCloud to use:

```
mysql -uroot -p
mysql> create database owncloud;
 mysql> grant all privileges on owncloud.* to "oc-user"@"localhost"
identified by "myrandompassword";
mysql> flush privileges;
```

MySQL is now ready to use. We just need to open ownCloud URL in a browser, and click on the **Advanced** link. Here we'll get an option to choose MySQL instead of SQLite. Fill in the required details and ownCloud will be ready to use.

ownCloud Setup with MySQL Configuration

Summary

Installing ownCloud is quite easy. It supports all the major operating systems without any hassle. All we need to have is a web server which can process PHP and a database. ownCloud provides an option to use SQLite or MySQL, both of which are easy to configure, and serve a distinct purpose. Now that our ownCloud instance is up and running, we can move forward and check out some features of ownCloud.

2
Usage of ownCloud and its Apps

ownCloud comes with a rich collection of apps. These are basically plugins that can be used to enhance ownCloud's functionality for a particular task. If we want to keep our ownCloud installation lean and simple, then we can just turn off all the apps, but then we will be losing a lot of things that ownCloud can do. We can see a list of available apps, along with the ones that are activated, by clicking on the drop-down list from the upper-right corner, and then selecting **Apps** from the menu. Here we can enable or disable any app by clicking on it, and then choosing the right option. We will now discuss some basic usage of ownCloud along with some very common apps.

Uploading a file

Uploading a file is the most basic functionality of ownCloud. We need to login before uploading a file. Once logged in we will see the New button with an upward arrow:

Clicking that arrow will show a system dialogue box for selecting and uploading files. We can choose multiple files, and upload them in one pass if we want by keeping the *Ctrl* key pressed. A status bar also appears next to the files that are being uploaded.

At times, we may want to transfer a file directly from a web server. We don't have to download it on a local computer, and then manually upload it to the ownCloud. We can just click on the **New** button, and then choose **From url** from the drop-down menu and paste the URL in the text field. ownCloud will pull the file from the web and store it.

Syncing and sharing a file

ownCloud has great syncing clients and capabilities. Desktop clients exist for Windows, Linux, and Mac. Android and iPhone clients are there to make sure that we can always access data even on the move. ownCloud supports two-way syncing, which means that changes done anywhere will propagate across all the devices associated with a particular account.

Installing and configuring ownCloud sync clients

Firstly, we need to download appropriate sync client for the platform from the following link:

```
http://owncloud.org/sync-clients/
```

To install the Linux client, we need to add ownCloud client repository first, and then install the client command line.

Ubuntu

Ubuntu users can install the ownCloud sync client by following the given commands:

```
# echo 'deb http://download.opensuse.org/repositories/isv:ownCloud:devel/
xUbuntu_12.04/ /' >> /etc/apt/sources.list.d/owncloud-client.list
# apt-get update
# apt-get install owncloud-client
```

Fedora

Steps to install ownCloud sync client for Fedora are quite similar to Ubuntu as follows:

```
# cd /etc/yum.repos.d/
# wget http://download.opensuse.org/repositories/isv:ownCloud:devel/
Fedora_17/isv:ownCloud:devel.repo
# yum install owncloud-client
```

Once we have installed the client, we need to run it on the terminal, which will produce a system dialogue box, as shown in the following screenshot:

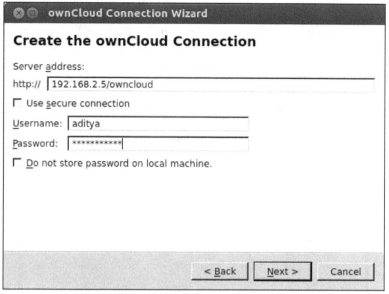

ownCloud Connection Wizard on Ubuntu

Once we fill in the details, such as the **Server address**, the client would be up and running. Server address is the URL which we use to access ownCloud web interface. By default, the sync directory is created in the home directory of the user who ran the ownCloud setup. Anything placed in this sync directory will be propagated to the ownCloud server as well as other devices associated with the same ownCloud user account.

Windows and Mac

For Windows and Mac, we just need to download the setup and run it. A dialogue box similar to the one in Linux will appear, and will install the sync client quickly.

At its core, ownCloud uses the **CSync** syncing engine that reads file metadata, and the modification timestamp in particular, to determine the last changes and propagate it through all the devices. CSync is lightweight, and does not need a specialized server component, which makes it ideal for all the platforms ownCloud supports.

ownCLoud Windows Client on Windows XP

Creating and editing text files

ownCloud makes it really easy to create and edit text files. We don't have to install any plugin for this, because editing is supported out of the box. Let us now create a file. We need to click on the familiar **New** button and then click on **Text file**. The **Text file** option will get converted into a field where we can enter the name of the file.

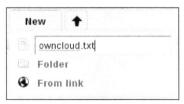

The file creation menu

Once we write the name of the file, and click on **return**, the file will be created. Now to edit the file, we need to click on the file created, and it will open in a text editor. It is a simple and lightweight editor. We can provide the text we want, and then click on the **Save** button to save the text.

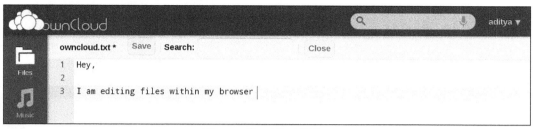

The ownCloud Text Editor

To make our lives easier, ownCloud maintains a changelog of the text files. Every time we save the file, ownCloud creates a backup point to which we can revert at any point in time. The backup points appear on the ownCloud's homepage in the form of **History** as we hover over the name of the file. If we click on **History**, a drop-down list will appear showing all the backup points created. We can select any one of these, and the file will be restored at that particular time. For example, we started editing the files and saved the file a few times, so our **History** drop-down list looks like the following screenshot:

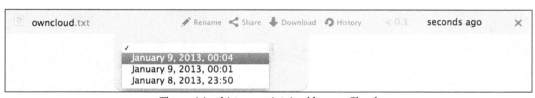

The revision history maintained by ownCloud

Sharing files using ownCloud

Sharing files with ownCloud is quite a simple process. We just have to hover over the file we want to share and the options will appear. If we want to share with an ownCloud user, we can just enter the user ID of the person, and the invite will be sent. In case the person is not on ownCloud, we can just create a link, and then share it using further options. ownCloud also allows us to password protect the files we want to share. We can also set an expiration date, after which the shared document will automatically become private again. All these features make the sharing experience very secure and ideal for confidential files.

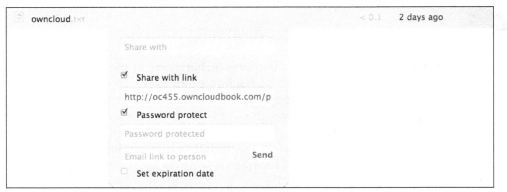

owncloud file sharing menu

Using ownCloud calendar

The following screenshot shows the ownCloud Calender app:

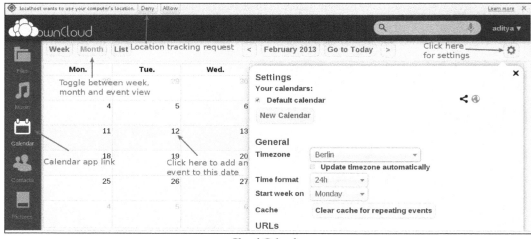

ownCloud Calendar app

ownCloud comes with a great calendar app. It runs a CalDAV server, such that any CalDAV compatible application can access and synchronize with ownCloud. CalDAV is an extension to WebDAV that uses `iCalendar` format for the data allowing multiple clients to access information easily and simultaneously. This means that events added on the ownCloud calendar can be easily synced with other apps, such as Apple Calendar app or Android CalDAV-Sync apps. The app can be accessed from the left side bar by clicking on the **Calendar** link. Once we click on it, ownCloud will ask the permission to track our location. This is used to set the time zone, and it is absolutely fine to deny the permission, and then set it manually using the small gear icon on the right corner of the interface. A default calendar is already created for every user but, of course, we can create more. It is generally a good idea to organize our calendars as personal and work. This way we can share our work calendar with our colleagues and our personal calendar with our friends and family members.

Let us create a calendar and name it as `work`. We have to click on the gear icon at upper right corner. This will display a menu where we can put the name of the calendar and choose a color for highlighting the tasks. Click on the **Save** button and a new calendar will be created. Now we can add events to it by clicking on any date.

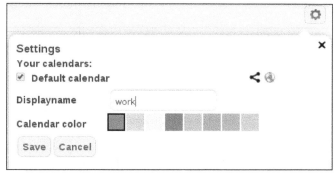

ownCloud Calendar creation menu

With ownCloud calendar we can do the following:

- Add events for the whole day
- Add events for a particular time slot
- Categorize the events in different calendars or within the same calendar
- Set up location and description of the events
- Set up recurrence of the events. This is useful to remind birthdays and periodic events such as taking medicine.

Everything mentioned can be done just by clicking any date on the calendar.

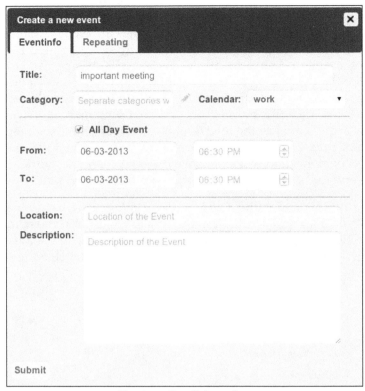

Create a new event ✕

| Eventinfo | Repeating |

Title: important meeting

Category: Separate categories w ✎ Calendar: work ▼

☑ All Day Event

From: 06-03-2013 06:30 PM ⬍

To: 06-03-2013 06:30 PM ⬍

Location: Location of the Event

Description: Description of the Event

Submit

Event creation dialogue box

In case we have to synchronize the events on the computer, we can easily do that using the `iCalender` link that can be obtained by clicking on the gear icon on upper right corner. Once we have the link, we can use any desktop or mobile app, such as Mozilla Sunbird, Mozilla Thunderbird, Evolution, Kontact, Microsoft Outlook, Apple Calendar, and so on to synchronize the events. Let us try using Mozilla Sunbird, because it is available for all the major operating systems, such as Linux, Windows, and Mac, and it is open sourced under various licenses.

Download Sunbird from `http://www.mozilla.org/projects/calendar/sunbird/` and install it. Once installed, on the left side of the application, there will be a tab displaying Calendars. Right-click on the empty area there, and navigate to **New Calendar**, and then select the **On the network** radio button. It then asks for the format, select **iCalnder**, and it provides the URL obtained from the ownCloud's gear icon. We have to name the calendar in the next screen and we are done. All the events will be downloaded, and any changes made on the ownCloud calendar will reflect on this calendar, keeping us updated about the events.

In case we do not want to subscribe to the calendar in the way we just did, we can download the entire event list in the form of iCal, and then import it in any calendar application, such as Sunbird. To download the calendar from ownCloud, just click on the small calendar icon next to the gear icon in upper right corner, and then hover over the calendar title. Here we can click on the down arrow button, and download the calendar that can be used to import any desktop app or any other ownCloud instance.

Using ownCloud contacts

ownCloud comes with a feature-packed contacts app. It lets you manage your contacts very easily, still giving you the capabilities to sync and import data. We can find contacts on the left sidebar of ownCloud. Contact app has a few pre-built groups that help in organizing our contacts from the very beginning. More groups can be added easily by clicking on the **New Group** button, and then filling in the name in a text field. A special group name, such as **All**, holds all the contacts of the address book. Let's create our first contact. We have to click on the **New Contact** button at the top of the page. A form for a new contact will appear where we can start by entering the name, e-mail, or phone number. We can set an image for the person. Additional fields, such as birthday, organization, and website can also be added by clicking on the **Add** drop-down menu at the bottom of the form.

Adding a new contact

Alternatively, we can import a .vcf file to add a number of contacts instantaneously. This enables us to export contacts from popular e-mail providers, such as Gmail, and import them to ownCloud.

It is also possible to export all your contacts in .vcf format and use it in other applications, such as Gmail and Kontact. All we need to do for this is to click on the small gear icon, and then click on the downwards arrow link to download. The downloaded .vcf can be uploaded to Gmail by clicking on the **Export** link in the **contacts** section of Gmail.

Syncing with smartphones is also easy with the in-built CardDav server provided by ownCloud. CardDAV is based on WebDAV, just like CalDAV, and is used to access the address books on remote servers. It uses .vcf format to handle contact data. For ownCloud installations, the CardDav URL looks like the following link:

```
http://owncloud.example.com/remote.php/carddav/
```

We can get the full URL easily by clicking on the CardDAV icon, next to the download icon, visible after clicking on the gear icon. If we want to synchronize to Apple devices, we have to use slightly modified version of the servers exposed at http://owncloud.example.com/remote.php/carddav/principals/username.

Let us try to sync our address book with an android phone. We will try an app named CardDAV-Sync from the Google Play store. After downloading it from the Google Play store, we just have to enter the CardDAV URL and the credentials for ownCloud user account. The app will then retrieve the address books stored with the ownCloud and display them. We can choose to sync only a few of the address books, and then click on **Finish**. All our contacts will be synced with the phone in no time. Desktop applications can be synced in a similar way.

Android CardDAV-Sync app

Viewing and sharing photographs

ownCloud lets us upload, and share images and photographs with our family and friends easily through the in-built photo gallery. All we have to do is upload the photographs and share the links to them. Let us try the same in a more practical manner. Let us first create a directory named my awesome trip, and upload some photographs there. Once this is done, we can go to the **Pictures** section by clicking on the left sidebar. A new collection called my awesome trip will appear there. We can click on this collection, and then on individual photographs. We can use arrow keys or a mouse scroll wheel to navigate through the photographs. Alternatively, we can watch a slideshow of all the photographs by clicking on the **slideshow** button on top left.

Sharing this collection is also easy with help of ownCloud. We have to basically share the folder. Just hover over the folder, and click on the **share** button. The familiar sharing interface will appear. We can choose the sharing parameters, such as **sharing with a URL**, **setting a password**, or **setting expiration date to the share**. Anyone can use the URL, and see the photographs. ownCloud also gives an option to download them as a `.zip` file, which is great for people who don't have an ownCloud account, or haven't synced their existing accounts locally.

Listening to music and watching videos

We can store and play songs and videos directly from the ownCloud interface. We just have to upload the songs and click on them. ownCloud music player will immediately play them, and you can see the player controls in the **Music** section in left sidebar.

Enabling the apps

Playing videos will require us to enable the video player app from the **Apps** menu. We can do this by clicking on the drop-down menu at the top right corner of the interface, and then selecting **Apps**. We have to find **Video Viewer** from the list of apps and enable it. After this, we can upload any video and watch it online by just clicking on it.

Summary

ownCloud has some really amazing apps. It comes pre-enabled with some most common apps, such as Text Editor, Calendar, and Address book with options to install many more. In addition, ownCloud gives us complete functionality to integrate it with other apps following CalDAV and CardDAV standards. Playing common music files and videos is also very easy, which increases their portability. In all, the options for customization are limited only by our imagination and PHP!

3
User Management and Admin Tools

Needless to say, users are the most important part of ownCloud ecosystem, and with users there is a need of user management. A good user management suite will help us to manage our ownCloud instance with less effort, and will help in providing a better user experience. Integrating ownCloud with other existing systems is the need of many industries today, and ownCloud user management plays a vital role here.

Inbuilt user and group management

ownCloud comes with strong user management features, inbuilt. Not only can we create users, but also we can put them into groups and set various controls over them. We are going to discuss some common things in this section. Grouping is an important feature, which eases the overall management tasks. We can create groups and have several groups, admins, and delegate responsibilities. We can adjust the disk quota, and fairly share it among our users, making life easier for everyone.

Creating users and groups

To create users, we have to click on the familiar drop-down menu at the top right corner and select **Users** option from there. This will open the user management console from where we are going to add the users. On the top we can see two empty fields for Login Name and Password. For user creation, we fill these fields. There is a drop-down for choosing the group next to it, where we can select the group appropriately.

In case a new group has to be created for better user management, we can do so by clicking on the last option, which is **add group**.

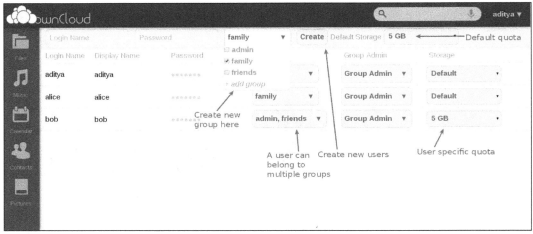

The User Management interface

Default storage

Often, we may want to prevent users from taking up too much space. Especially in corporate environments, where there are a lot of users, over consumption of system resources like disk, can cause system slowdown. Other users might also get affected by them. ownCloud lets us define user quotas easily, so that we can limit the usage of space per user. This can be set by using the drop-down next to every user in user management console. Alternatively, we can set each user to an option of default, and then set **Default** quota from the top drop-down. There are certain pre-set values, but we have the flexibility to set the quota to any arbitrary number. By default, the minimum quota is 1 GB.

Integrating ownCloud with LDAP

Bigger organizations tend to deploy a directory server for user management. **Lightweight Directory Protocol (LDAP)** is the most widely used standard for maintaining distributed directory information services over an **Internet Protocol (IP)** network. **OpenLDAP** and **Active Directory** are widely used implementations of LDAP, and we are going to integrate them with ownCloud. We will see how the implementation of OpenLDAP can be configured on a bare CentOS. We will also setup basic Active Directory on Windows Server 2008, and we will integrate them both with ownCloud. Digging into intricacies of OpenLDAP and Active Directory is not feasible for this book, but we'll walk through a basic setup.

Installing LDAP user and group backend

Before we begin installing LDAP servers, we need to enable LDAP support at ownCloud. It can be easily done by enabling **LDAP user and group backend** application from **Apps** menu.

Now, let us go to the **Admin** page and check out the configuration parameters provided by LDAP.

- **Server configuration**: A dropdown list of saved server configurations, ideal for testing.
- **Host**: The hostname of the machine where LDAP server is running. It can be an IP address if LDAP is configured that way.
- **Base DN**: The base DN of LDAP. All the users and groups should be accessible from here.
- **User DN**: The User DN of the user who can perform searches on the LDAP.
- **Password**: The password for the user as defined in User DN field.
- **User Login Filter**: The filter to use when a user tries to login. Use %uid as placeholder for the username.
- **User List Filter**: The filter to use when a search for users will be executed.
- **Group Filter**: The filter to use when a search for groups will be executed.

The first five are used all the time, even for the simplest installations, such as ours. We can omit the last two for now.

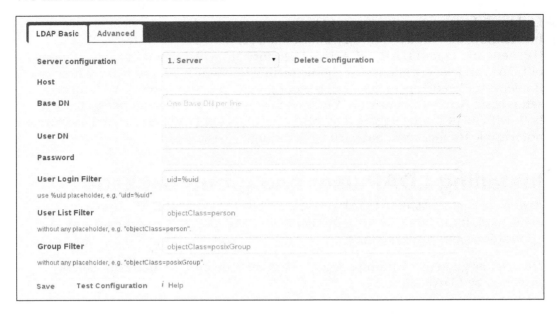

We can also try to configure the **Advanced** option, but it is recommended to leave it at default, unless we have a good reason to change it. This interface allows the user to change the connection settings as shown in the following screenshot:

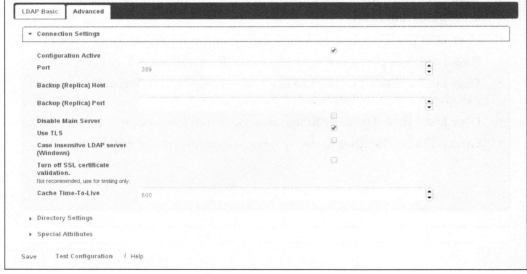

The Connection Settings tab

The **Directory Settings** tab will let us define various LDAP tree and search attributes as shown in the following screenshot:

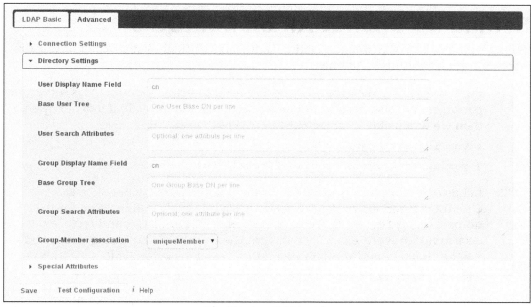

The Directory Settings tab

The following screenshot shows the **Special Attributes** interface:

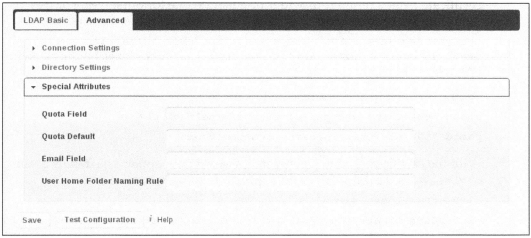

The Special Attributes tab

The LDAP **Advanced** setting tab can be used to define several advanced parameters, which are usually optional and non-default port number and quota.

Setting up OpenLDAP on CentOS 6

Setting up OpenLDAP with basic setting is not very difficult. We can just follow the steps and get it running in no time:

1. First, we will lay the groundwork. We need to install OpenLDAP's server packages. We also need to unblock port 389 of the firewall, if it is not open, then we will install `system-config-firewall-tui` package.

    ```
    # yum install openldap-servers
    # yum install system-config-firewall-tui
    ```

2. Let us configure the OpenLDAP for the domain `owncloudbook.com`. OpenLDAP-servers package already has a minimal configuration for the domain `example.com`. Open `olcDatabase={2}bdb.ldif`, and replace the occurrence of word `example` with `owncloudbook`. We are going to use `sed` for this, but `vim` and similar other editors can be used as well.

    ```
    sed -i "s/example/owncloudbook/g" olcDatabase={2}bdb.ldif
    ```

    Even though we have changed the config without even opening the file, it is advisable to have a look at it and try to understand the different parameters.

3. We also need to provide it with a certificate for TLS. We can use a signed certificate from a reputed provider or generate one for ourselves. For this demo, we will generate one.

    ```
    openssl req -new -x509 -nodes -out /etc/pki/tls/certs/
    owncloudbook-cert.pem -keyout /etc/pki/tls/certs/owncloudbook-key.
    pem -days 3650
    ```

4. Set the ownership and permission bits for these two files:

    ```
    chown root:ldap /etc/pki/tls/certs/owncloudbook*
    chmod 750 /etc/pki/tls/certs/owncloudbook*
    ```

5. With the certificate and key generated, we can now append its details to the `olcDatabase={2}bdb.ldif` and supply a Root password as well.

    ```
    olcRootPW: somepassword
    olcTLSCertificateFile: /etc/pki/tls/certs/owncloudbook-cert.pem
    olcTLSCertificateKeyFile: /etc/pki/tls/certs/owncloudbook-key.pem
    ```

6. We have to change the occurrence of `example.com` for `olcDatabase={1}` `monitor.ldif` as well.

   ```
   sed -i "s/example/owncloudbook/g" olcDatabase={1}monitor.ldif
   ```

7. We need a bare minimum database config for our installation. An example config is provided with `openldap-servers` package. We will copy that to the appropriate directory and set the right ownership.

   ```
   cp /usr/share/openldap-servers/DB_CONFIG.example /var/lib/ldap/
   DB_CONFIG
   ```
   ```
   chown -Rf ldap:ldap /var/lib/ldap/
   ```

8. We also have to turn on the TLS from `sysconfig`.

   ```
   vim /etc/sysconfig/ldap
   ```
   ```
   SLAPD_LDAPS=yes
   ```

9. Now just test the configuration by running `slaptest`.

   ```
   slaptest -u
   ```

10. If the config passes, start the service.

    ```
    services lapd start
    ```

11. Since we used self-signed certificates, we need to append the following to `ldap` configuration file:

    ```
    TLS_CACERT /etc/pki/tls/certs/owncloudbook-cert.pem
    ```
    ```
    URI ldap://127.0.0.1
    ```
    ```
    BASE dc=owncloudbook,dc=com
    ```

12. Fire up an `ldapsearch` to see if it worked:

    ```
    ldapsearch -x  -b "dc=owncloudbook,dc=com"
    ```

13. Let's add some groups and users. We will create the files `base.ldif`, `groups.ldif` and `users.ldif` to schema.

    ```
    vim /etc/openldap/schema/base.ldif
    ```
    ```
    dn: dc=owncloudbook,dc=com
    ```
    ```
    dc: owncloudbook
    ```
    ```
    objectClass: top
    ```
    ```
    objectClass: domain
    ```

    ```
    dn: ou=Users,dc=owncloudbook,dc=com
    ```
    ```
    ou: Users
    ```
    ```
    objectClass: top
    ```

```
objectClass: organizationalUnit


dn: ou=Group,dc=owncloudbook,dc=com
ou: Group
objectClass: top
objectClass: organizationalUnit


vim /etc/openldap/schema/group.ldif
dn: cn=ocuser1,ou=Group,dc=owncloudbook,dc=com
objectClass: posixGroup
objectClass: top
cn: ocuser1
userPassword: password
gidNumber: 1000


vim /etc/openldap/schema/users.ldif
dn: uid=ocuser1,ou=Users,dc=owncloudbook,dc=com
uid: ocuser1
cn: ocuser1
objectClass: account
objectClass: posixAccount
objectClass: top
objectClass: shadowAccount
userPassword: password
shadowLastChange: 15140
shadowMin: 0
shadowMax: 99999
shadowWarning: 7
loginShell: /bin/bash
uidNumber: 1000
gidNumber: 1000
homeDirectory: /home/ocuser1
```

14. Now execute the `ldif` files so that these users get added to our `ldap` server:

```
ldapadd -xc -W -D "cn=Manager,dc=owncloudbook,dc=com" -f base.ldif

ldapadd -xc -W -D "cn=Manager,dc=owncloudbook,dc=com" -f group.ldif

ldapadd -xc -W -D "cn=Manager,dc=owncloudbook,dc=com" -f users.ldif
```

We run the same search command again, and see that new users have appeared. The OpenLDAP server is ready.

Integrating ownCloud with OpenLDAP

To integrate ownCloud with OpenLDAP that we just configured, we need to make appropriate entries in the Admin section. We have to click on the tiny gear icon at the bottom left, and go to the Admin area. There we would see the **LDAP configuration** menu. We just need to put in the right details, and click on **Test Configuration**. Once the configuration is passed, we can click on the **Save** button, and OpenLDAP would be ready to use with ownCloud.

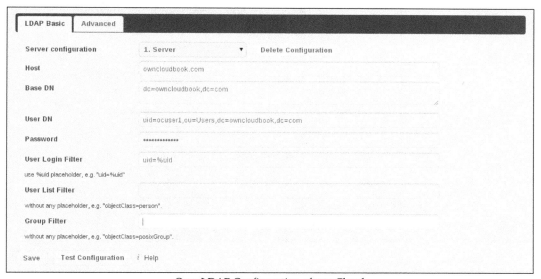

OpenLDAP Configuration of ownCloud

Setting up Active Directory on Windows Server 2008

Active Directory can be implemented on any of the Windows machines. We will set up an Active Directory server on Windows 2008 Server.

1. Similar to IIS installation, we need to configure an Active Directory role for the server. For that we need to go to **Server Manager** application from the **Start** menu. From **Server Manager** application, we have to choose **Add Roles** link on the right side of the application.

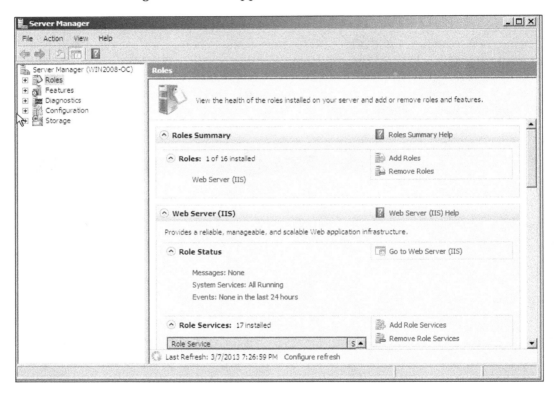

2. We will be presented with a set of checkboxes, where we can select the roles for the server. Here we will choose **Active Directory Domain Services** as the role and click on the **Next** button.

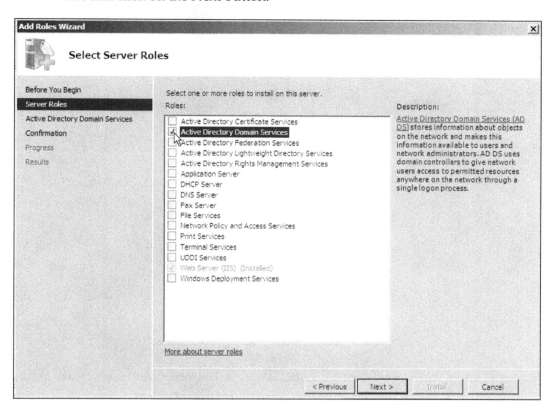

3. The next screen will show us some helpful pointers. We can read them, and then click on the **Next** button.

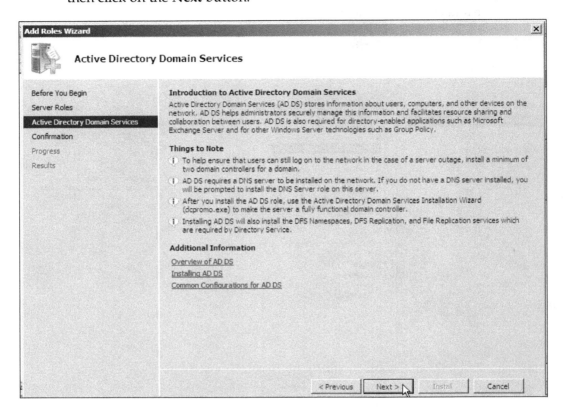

4. A confirmation dialogue box will appear. Again, read through it and click on the **Install** button.

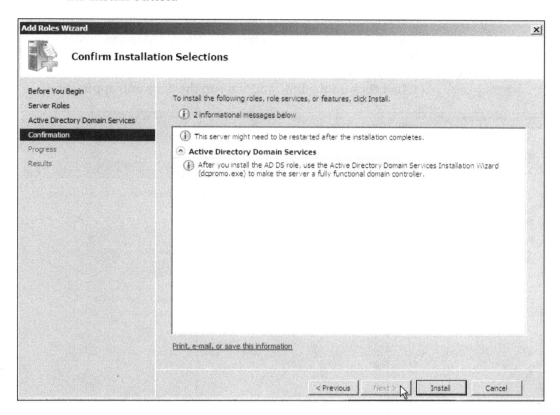

Finally, it is going to install the AD service. It may take a few minutes for this, and may prompt for a restart. It is advisable to restart immediately after the AD installation anyway.

1. Once the machine reboots, we have to go to the **Server Manager** again from the **Start** menu. Here we would see an information message stating that **The server is not running as the domain controller**, and we need to run `dcpromo.exe`. Just click on the link, and it'll run the dcpromo application.

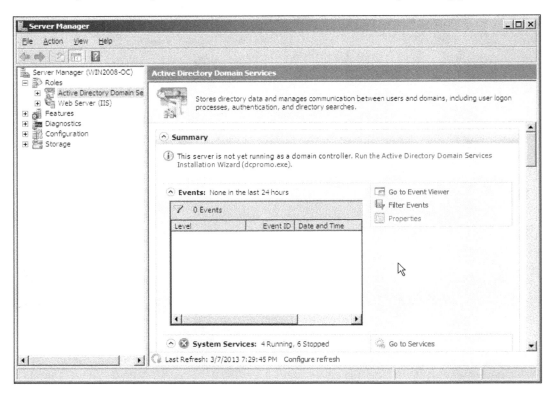

2. The **Active Directory Domain Services Installation Wizard** will open. We just have to click on the **Next** button here.

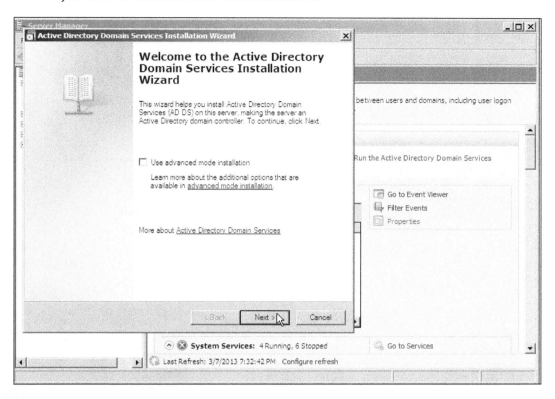

3. An informational message with some text about the compatibility will appear. We can read through it, and click on the **Next** button.

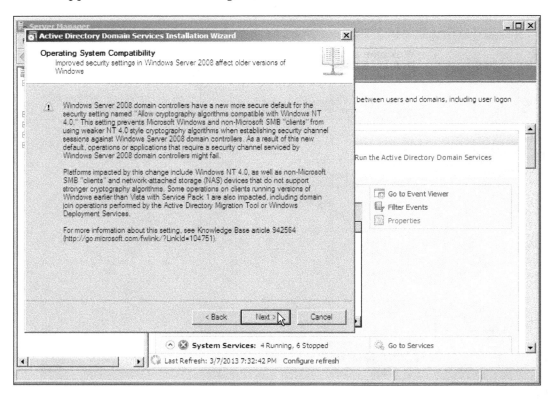

4. The next screen will give an option to add the server to an existing domain forest or to create a new domain in a new forest. Now the first radio button, **Existing forest**, is used when we want to add the server to an existing implementation of Active Directory. There are more options to consider here. For this example, we will go with **Create a new domain in a new forest**.

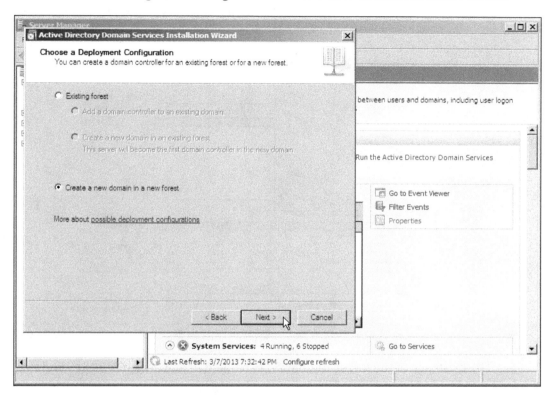

5. We need to give a **Fully Qualified Domain Name (FQDN)** in this screen. We will use `owncloudbook.com` for this example, and click on the **Next** button.

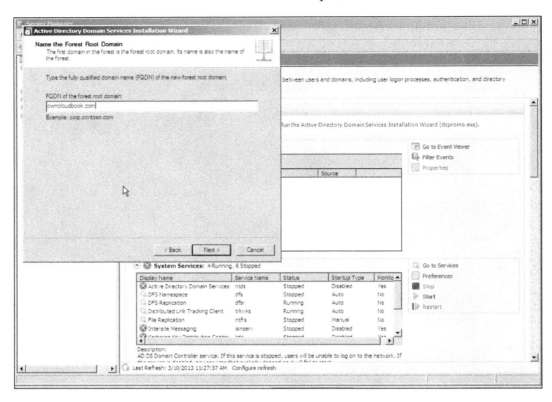

6. The existence of the forest and NetBIOS name will be verified in next window.

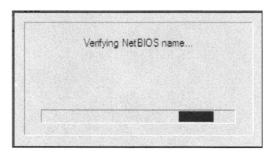

7. Now the wizard will ask you for the functional level of the Active Directory. In simple terms it means the compatibility. If we want to add an older version of Windows, we will choose it or go with Windows 2008, if our Domain forest consists of only Windows 2008 Server. We will choose Windows Server 2008 here, and click on the **Next** button.

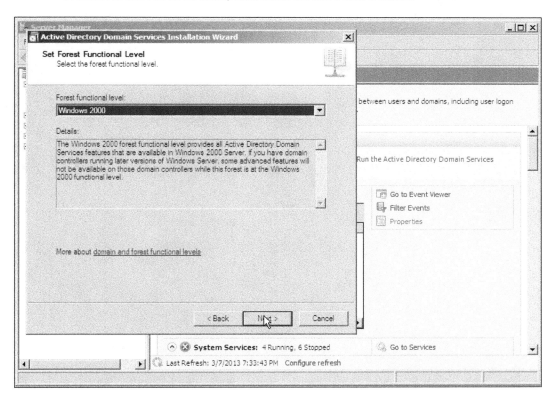

8. In the next screen, we get to choose additional options for the **Domain Controller**. Because this is going to be the only server in the forest for this domain, we will make this the **DNS server**.

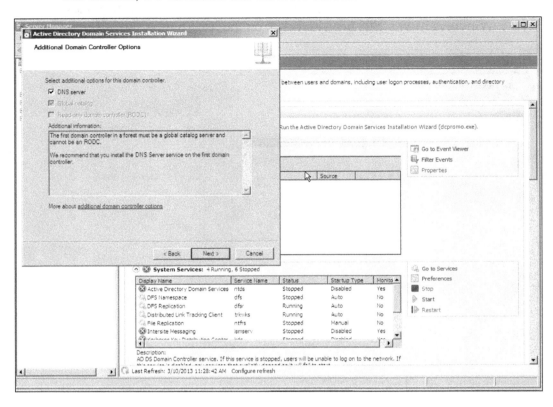

9. It may throw up an error if it fails to detect an authoritative parent zone, but we don't need to worry, because we can configure this manually later. Right now, we just have to click on the **Yes** button.

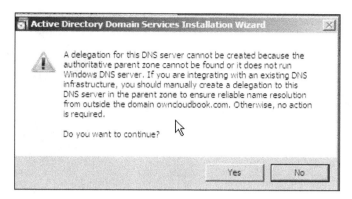

10. The next screen will let us choose NTDS database location. The defaults would be good here for smaller installations.

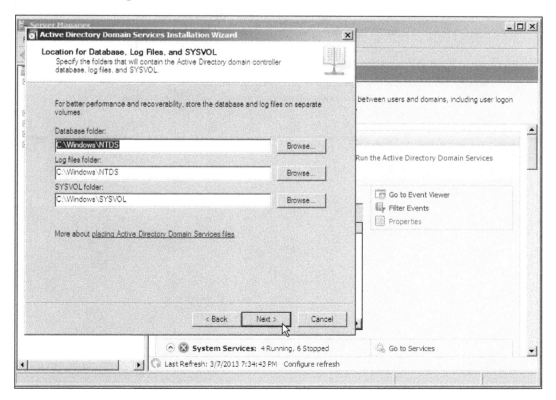

11. We will be shown a summary of the entire process. Click on the **Next** button, and the installation will begin. It may take a few minutes. It is advisable to reboot after this.

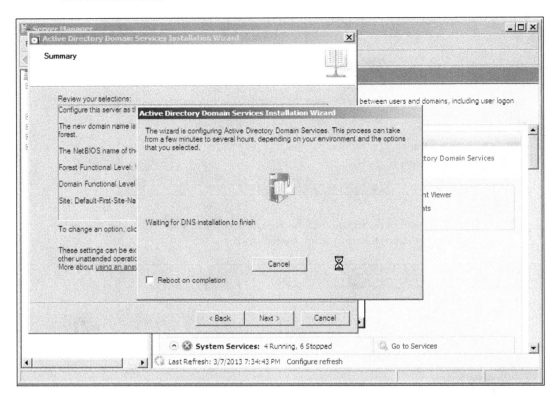

12. Now we need to create some users on this Active Directory. Just go to the **Start** menu and click on **Administrative Tools**. We will see **Active Directory Users and Computers**, which we have to click.

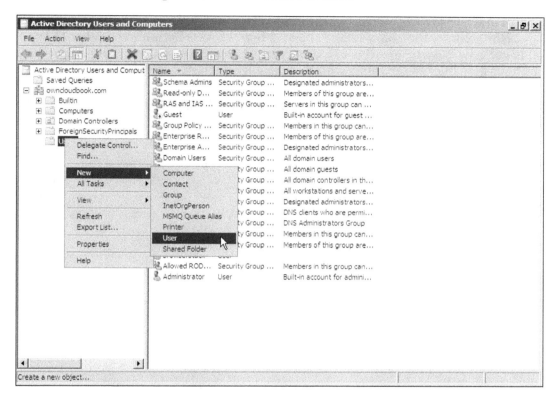

Here we can create more users and groups easily by a GUI dialogue box.

Once the users are created, it is a good idea to test the Active Directory using Dsquery (http://technet.microsoft.com/en-us/library/cc732952.aspx) command line tool.

```
C:\Users\Administrator>dsquery user
"CN=Administrator,CN=Users,DC=owncloudtest,DC=com"
"CN=Guest,CN=Users,DC=owncloudtest,DC=com"
"CN=krbtgt,CN=Users,DC=owncloudtest,DC=com"
"CN=ocuser1,CN=Users,DC=owncloudtest,DC=com"
"CN=ocuser10,CN=Users,DC=owncloudtest,DC=com"
```

Integrating Active Directory with ownCloud

Similar to OpenLDAP, this configuration also has to be done at Admin page of the ownCloud. Just go to Admin page, and fill up the LDAP configuration form as shown in the following screenshot. Additionally, we have to go to the **Advanced** tab of the configuration, and set the **Group-Member Association** to **member (AD)**, and check the **Case insensitive LDAP server (Windows)** check box. We can test the configuration once we are done, and then save it if the test is successful.

LDAP configuration is used for Active Directory as well

Other admin tasks

As an administrator of the ownCloud instance, we have to deal with some more issues. We need to configure the options provided in the Admin page to suit the need of our users. Let us discuss these issues and options briefly one by one.

- **Enable ZIP-download**: Turning this on will let our users create compressed ZIP archives and download more than one file easily. Now, ideally we would always want to have this option enabled, but remember that creating a ZIP archive consumes CPU cycles. So, if we are running tight on CPU, then probably we can save some processing time by turning this off.

- **File Versioning**: Again we would want this to be enabled for everyone, but keep in mind that this will consume more space on the disk, because ownCloud will maintain different versions of the files.

- **Cron**: There are certain maintenance tasks which ownCloud does using cron jobs, such as updating cache from LDAP or checking for updates. We can configure the way cron should run. Usually, a default works the best for everyone.

- **Sharing**: ownCloud is all about controlling your own data and freedom. If the data is not sensitive, we would want all the sharing options to be turned on, but for corporates who really want to protect their data, there is an option to turn off sharing and related features.

Summary

ownCloud provides us with powerful features for user management and admin tasks. This helps us to make sure that the system resources are well utilized and distributed among the users, and no user should be able to exploit the instance and disrupt the services.

Integrating with popular LDAP services is quite easy and eases the task of the administrator. This also helps in corporate environment, where there are services such as OpenLDAP or Active Directory already present, saving hours of admin work to create users and set quotas manually.

4
Securing your ownCloud

The Internet is not the safest place today. Everyday, we hear about websites getting hacked, software reporting vulnerabilities, and servers getting compromised. We need to protect ourselves and the data we possess. In this chapter we will focus on the security aspects of our setup. If we are putting anything on the Internet, then we have to make sure that our server is secure, and does not allow anyone to do anything unauthorized with malicious intent. It is worth noting that these guides, while helpful, are in no way exhaustive. System security is a very wide field, and new threats emerge everyday and get fixed.

Hardening the web server

Web server is the most important component of the ownCloud setup. It is also one of the most likely targets of malicious hackers, because it is a public facing piece of the infrastructure. In this section, we will see how to make it really hard for the bad guys to penetrate through our ownCloud instance. We will first talk about hardening Apache web server, and then we will see some similar practice for IIS as well.

Apache hardening

Securing the web server is important, even if we plan to use our ownCloud installation for something non-personal and non-confidential, because if the security of our server is compromised, then it can be used to harm others, and we would be held responsible in most of the cases. Using some simple techniques, we can secure our Apache web server and give penetrators a hard time.

Linux comes with great users and group management commands and utilities. If used properly, these are some of the most powerful tools in hands of a system administrator. We should create a separate user and restrict it to the ownCloud installation directory. Apache will run as this user.

```
useradd -d /var/www/ocroot ocwebuser
```

Now, we will extract the ownCloud tar archive downloaded from ownCloud.org in /var/www/ocroot, and install it there. Even if we have an ownCloud instance already running, it is fine to execute the preceding useradd command. We just need to ensure that ocwebsuer owns the files in it.

```
chown -R ocwebuser /var/www/ocroot
```

After extracting the tar archive, a directory with ownCloud source, named owncloud, will be there. This directory will be our document root for Apache. Now we will create a data directory for storing the data uploaded by the users. We can also put SQLite in this directory if we want.

```
mkdir /var/www/ocroot/ocdata
```

Once we are done configuring the home of ocwebuser, it should look like this:

```
ls -l /var/www/ocroot
total 8
drwxrwxr-x 2 ocwebuserocwebuser 4096 Feb  3 11:54 ocdata
drwxrwxr-x 2 ocwebuserocwebuser 4096 Feb  3 11:54 owncloud
```

Now, we should also make sure that this user has no access to shell for security reasons. This restriction will make sure that even if somehow we have a security breach, ocwebuser will not be able to execute any shell commands. We can either edit the /etc/passwd file or simple execute the following command:

```
usermod -s /bin/false ocwebuser
```

We should also lock the account of the ocwebuser by scrambling the password.

```
passwd -l ocwebuser
```

This option is available to root only. This renders the encrypted password to an invalid string. Try logging in using `ocwebuser`, and it should fail.

Now open the `apache.conf` or `httpd.conf`, and find the section where **User** is defined. Edit it to make `ocwebuser` apache user, and restart Apache.

```
User ocwebuser
Group ocwebuser
```

We would also set the `ServerToken` parameter to `prod`. This makes sure that apache reveals minimum information about its version and operating system. This reduces, but does not eliminate, the chances of getting compromised by version specific vulnerabilities.

```
ServerToken prod
```

We have done some basic stuff to make our Apache server a bit more secure than the usual.

IIS hardening

IIS, as we know, is a well-known web server for Windows platform. In this section, we will discuss some ways to secure it for production environments.

UrlScan

UrlScan is a tool by Microsoft that scans all the incoming URLs that IIS has to execute. This way, we can block the IIS user to read and execute only on this drive and remove all other permissions. It can block potential harmful requests and help in blocking SQL and code injections. We can modify the rules and adjust them as per our needs. Download UrlScan from `http://www.iis.net/downloads/microsoft/urlscan`. We should note here that by default, UrlScan applies globally, so if we are going to host more than one website on this server, then we may need to setup site specific filters. To setup a site filter, we need to copy `UrlScan.dll` and `UrlScan.ini` from the default location to the ownCloud directory. After this, in IIS Manager, look for ISAPI Filters, and then click on **Add**, and point the path to the `UrlScan.dll`.

Application pool identity

It was introduced in Windows Server 2008 Service Pack 2. Before this, all the network applications used to run with user NETWORKSERVICE, but as the number of applications grew, the potential risk of sharing the same user became obvious. If one of the applications got compromised, then it risked all other applications because they were running with the same user. With application pool identities, **IIS Admin Process (WAS)** will create a user account (virtual) dynamically for every Application Pool added with the name of the new Application Pool, and run the Application Pool's worker processes using this account. This happens automatically for IIS 7.5 onwards, but for older versions of IIS, this can be configured in IIS Management Console. Choose the site to be modified, and click on the **View Application Pools** on right sidebar.

Choose the **Application pool**, and click on the **Advanced Settings**. Here we
have to set **Identity** in the Process Model, and set it to **ApplicationPoolIdentity**
from **NetworkService**.

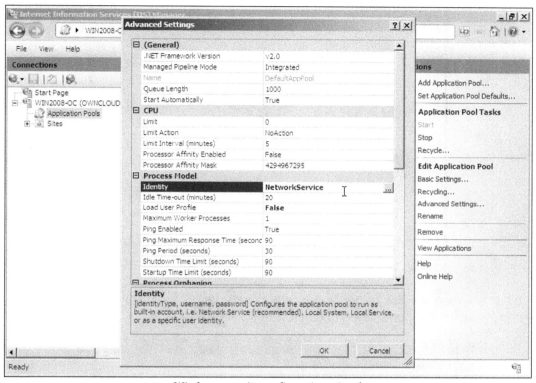

Windows security configuration wizard

This wizard can be used to lock down the Windows server in an easy way. Fair
warning though, if not configured carefully, it can actually stop even the legitimate
applications to run, or worse, it can lock us out and won't allow us to login.
We recommend that you try this on a staging machine first before applying to
production environment.

Open the **Security Configuration Wizard** from the **Start** menu. The wizard will appear in the welcome screen.

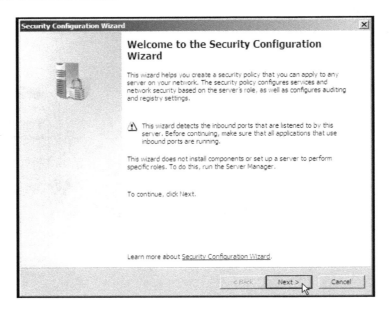

The next screen will ask us, if we want to create a new security policy or want to edit or apply an existing one. We will create a new security policy.

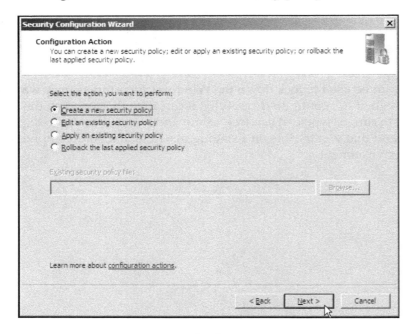

At the next screen, we have to specify the server name. If it is configured to a domain, we can use that, or we can go with the IP of the server. Because we are doing this on our local system, we will provide it an IP.

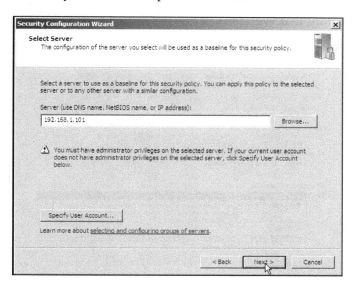

A processing dialogue box will appear with a status bar. It can take a minute for it to finish the processing. After this, we will be prompted to configure **Role-Based Service Configuration**. This is what we want to do. Because this machine will be running IIS, we need to configure it for that.

Next, the wizard will detect the installed roles, and will present us options to allow or stop them. Usually the wizard picks up the most suitable choices still we can go through the list and turn on anything we require or turn off anything we won't need.

We should make sure that **Web Server** role is selected here.

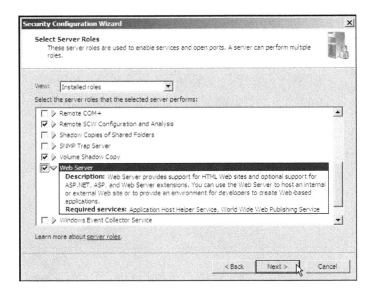

The next screen will present us the list of **Installed features**. This is also important, because a server is also client for various other services such as DNS.

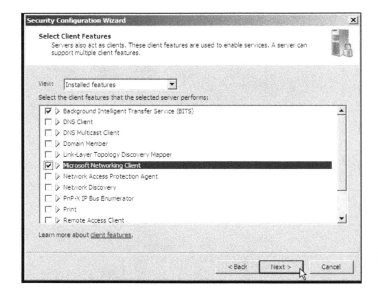

The next screen of the wizard will show the list of **Installed options**. Defaults are good here.

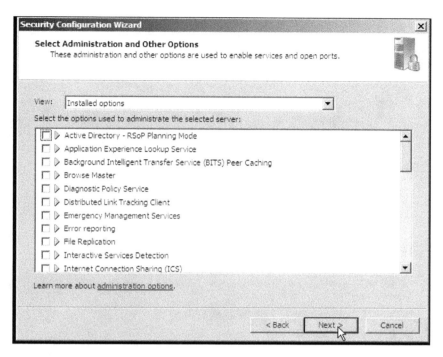

The next stage will ask us about what to do in case an unspecified service is encountered. We have set it to **Disable the service**, but again, it is better to test this before applying it on production.

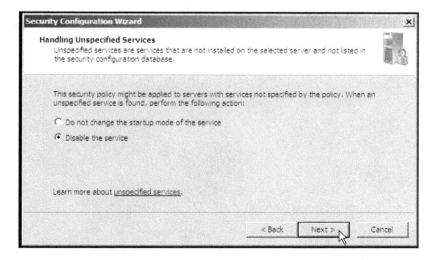

On the next screen, we will be asked to review the changes we are about to make in the services. It is very important to go through this and make sure that everything is in order.

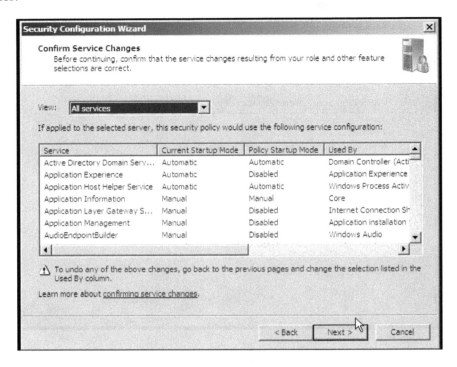

The next three screens will present us options to edit various policies of the server. Unless we really know what we are doing, we should not play around with these. They control various aspects, such as Network security, routing protocols, several registry settings, and audit policies. Although we have turned all several things on production instance, such as auditing all successful and unsuccessful activities, it is generally not required, and it is fine if these are skipped altogether.

Now that we have made all these changes, the wizard will ask for a location to save these settings. An XML file is created which can also be edited manually later.

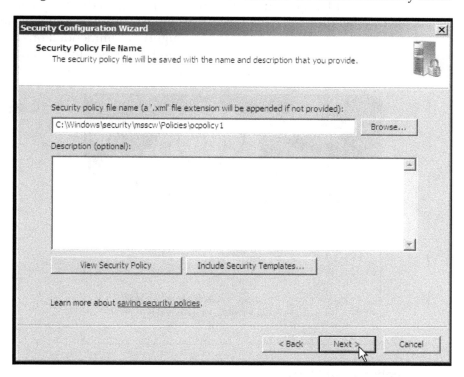

The next screen will prompt us to either apply the policy later or right away. Later is a good choice, if we are not sure and would like to review the XML first. If we are confident about the configurations, we can choose to apply it immediately.

Securing ownCloud data directory

When we install ownCloud, it gives us a warning about the data directory being accessible via the Internet directly. Now this can be a major problem and security threat. One way is to use `.htaccess`, but it is not a highly recommended one, because `.htaccess` is capable of doing much more, and if it gets into the hands of a wrong person, it can do huge damage to the data.

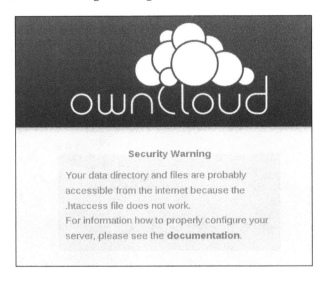

Our recommendation would be to disable `htaccess` altogether, and just move the data directory out of the web server's root. Going by the configuration we did before while hardening Apache, a location like `/var/www/ocroot/data` would be most secure. We should also ensure that permission of this directory is set as `700`.

```
chmod 700 /var/www/ocroot/data
```

Once the permission is set, just go to the advanced section while installing ownCloud, and put the preceding path there.

Path of data folder which should be changed

Security database

Database is very crucial for the operation of ownCloud. Among other things, the database holds login information for the user, including encrypted password. The security of the database becomes very critical for this reason.

For smaller instances where MySQL resides on the same box, we should always make sure that we bind MySQL server process on 127.0.0.1, instead of all the interfaces. This will ensure that network logins other than from the host machine itself will not be allowed, because the MySQL server will bind to the local interface only. We will add `bind-address` to [mysqld] section in `my.cnf` file for this.

```
bind-address=127.0.0.1
```

Alternatively, we can choose to stop MySQL from listening to any port by asking it to skip networking altogether.

```
skip-networking
```

If the MySQL used by ownCloud resides on some other host, then we have to take some additional steps to safe guard our MySQL server. This is generally the case with large organizations and institutions. We cannot do skip-networking here, because ownCloud is on another box, and it will need to make a network connection to connect to the MySQL database. One great way is to allow only the ownCloud IP to connect to the MySQL port, and drop rest of the connections. On Linux, this can be done using `iptables`.

```
iptables -I INPUT \! --srcx .x.x.x -m tcp -p tcp --dport 3306 -j DROP
```

We can use Windows firewall on Windows server.

We should remove all the extra things that comes with MySQL pre-packaged or the things which we may have created over the time, if it is an old MySQL installation. MySQL comes with a standard database named `test`. We should delete this database, because it is allowed anonymous access:

```
mysql> drop database test;
```

Also, it would be a good idea to take some time and go through the user list of MySQL, and remove all the users who no longer need database access.

```
mysql> select * from mysql.user;
```

Ensure that logging is enabled. We can study these logs for strange login patterns or unusual queries.

```
log =/var/log/mysql/mysql.log
```

We should stop MySQL from reading local files. This can be a life saver in case the MySQL got compromised, because it will prevent the penetrators from reading system critical files such as `/etc/passwd`.

```
local-infile=0
```

ownCloud encryption

The ownCloud 4.0 was released with a server-side encryption. Unfortunately, it was discovered after release that the encryption is not very strong. It was implemented using PHP's `mt_rand()` function, which is not a very strong random number generator. For encryption, the recommended entropy should be at least 80 bits, whereas using the ownCloud's implementation that time the maximum achievable entropy was about 68 bits only.

It was also pointed out that the keys were being stored in session in clear text, which increased the vulnerability of the encryption. Moreover, because the communication itself was not mandatorily over HTTPs, the chances of somebody snooping over the wire were also very high. In short, it may not be a good idea to store highly confidential data if you are running any older version than ownCloud 5.

Another point of concern was that ownCloud saved the keys in `/tmp` instead of memory. Because the keys were written to a physical disk, there were chances that it could be recovered by recovery tools, which further rendered ownCloud encryption to be unfit for a production environment.

Starting ownCloud 5.0.7, OpenSSL, which is much stronger, is used for encryption. We can enable this from the Apps page, and currently it does server-side encryption. Client-side encryption is still under works, and will be released soon. At the moment, it is not recommended to use this encryption in production, because it is still in beta/pre-release state.

Summary

We have learned some of the very basic techniques to make our ownCloud server a bit more secure. We saw how Apache and IIS can be hardened. We got some handy tips to secure MySQL too. We had a look at encryption with ownCloud, and saw the shortcomings of ownCloud 4.x encryption implementation, and what ownCloud 5 did to make it more secure.

Achieving a hundred percent safety is not possible in today's world, but these steps will reduce the vulnerabilities to a great extent, and help us in keeps our data safe.

5
ownCloud Backup, Restore, and Logging

This chapter is focused on the three important administrative tasks that play a vital role in disasters. Machines fail! No matter what kind of hardware we buy, there is always a chance that it will not work properly. Additionally, we have to account for human errors. Restoring from backups is the only options in many of such cases. Logging is useful for debugging and auditing the instance. Although these are absolutely required for production grade setups, having backups can be helpful for personal instance owners as well.

ownCloud backup

ownCloud is a PHP application, and like many other PHP applications out there, there are three important things which constitute ownCloud full backup.

- ownCloud config file
- ownCloud data directory
- ownCloud database

As an enterprise solution, **Bacula Network Backup Solution** (http://www.bacula.org/) is quite popular. It can run in fully distributed fashion, and can do much more than backing up ownCloud. It can work with the sophisticated storage backends such as RAID or network drives, as well as traditional backends such as tape drives. It can catalogue the backups, and presents an easy to understand the restore functionality.

The following are the important components of Bacula:

- **Bacula Director**: The Director service is responsible for defining and scheduling a backup task. It also defines the storage location and the data to be backed up.

- **Bacula File Daemon**: This service reads and verifies the files which are to be backed up. This service runs on all the clients, and it is responsible for sending the data to the storage service.

- **Bacula Storage Daemon**: The Storage Daemon receives the files from the File Daemon, and is responsible for the actual storage as per the configuration. It manages the various storage backends such as RAID or simple SATA hard disks and so on.

- **Bacula Console**: Console is the interface to communicate with Bacula Director. It can be used to create new tasks and to delete or modify the existing ones.

Bacula is a highly flexible and open source solution. We should consult Bacula documentation if we want to set it up for a large deployment.

For personal setups, where Bacula might be an overkill, all we have to do is copy the file to another remote location periodically or upon change. We can use scp or ftp for this.

```
scp owncloud/config/config.php aditya@remoteserver:/backups/conf
```

An arguably better solution could be to use a git repository for the file, so that we can get a version controlled history for config.php, but some administrators may find it overkill for just a single file. After all, we do not expect a config file to change very frequently.

For the backup of the data directory, it would be a good idea to archive the entire data directory periodically and send it to a remote location. Let's do this by putting a cron job to tar the data directory.

```
crontab -e
04 * * * tar -czvf datadir-`date +\%s`.tar.gz owncloud/data/;scp datadir-
`date +\%s`.tar.gz aditya@remoteserver:/backups/datadir
```

The preceding `crontab` entry will create a gzip archive every day at 4 a.m. in the morning. Additionally, the archive will be time stamped by using date command and passing `%s` flag. The character '\' is used as an escape character. It is not required, while running the command directly in bash shell. Once the data directory is archived then we `scp` it to a remote location. We prefer using `scp` over `ftp` and other mechanisms because it is way more secure, and key-based authentication eliminates the need of putting password manually or writing an expect script. Other mechanisms such as `rsync` can be used for transferring the backup of data directory, but we may not be saving a lot of bandwidth, since it is a new file, and not an incremental backup. If we just want incremental backups instead of full backups, then `rsync` is more desirable.

```
rsync -avz owncloud/data/ aditya@remoteserver:/backups/datadir
```

In case we send the data to a remote location, we should make sure that the data is transmitted securely, and the server where we are saving the data is secure. Also, it is a good idea to make users aware that their data is being archived and saved at another location.

Now let us look into the MySQL backup. We can use command line utility to take backups, or we can use MySQL workbench. We will see both the ways, but on production infrastructure command line utility is recommended, because it can be scripted to take the backups periodically. The command line tool we are going to see is shipped with standard MySQL server, and is known as `mysqldump`.

```
mysqldump -u ocdbuserownlcoud>owncloud-`date +%s`.sql
```

The previous command can be put in crontab as before and we can have our periodic backups, and upload them to a remote location using scp or any other mechanism.

We can also take backups using MySQL Workbench. It is a free tool, downloadable from MySQL's website (`http://www.mysql.com/downloads/workbench/`). Before running the installer, we recommend installing Visual C++ 2010 (`http://www.microsoft.com/download/details.aspx?id=5555`) and .Net Framework 4.0 Client Profile (`http://www.microsoft.com/download/details.aspx?id=24872`).

Once the installation of the MySQL Workbench is done, we can use it to create backups manually. We just have to open the Workbench, and choose appropriate MySQL server from the **Server Administration** panel in the right. Since, we have our MySQL on local machine; it says **Local MySQL** on our Workbench. In case we want it to connect it to a remote database, we would have clicked on the **New Server Instance** link in the **Server Administration**, and would have provided a hostname or IP address. After we choose the MySQL server, we have to click on the **Manage Import / Export link**. It'll prompt us for a password to access the database.

The Workbench will present a screen with the list of databases. Here, we will choose ownCloud database. Also, we want to choose **Export to Self-Contained File**, because this will create a single file for the entire database and restoring becomes much easier with this option. Once we are done with all this, we will click on the **Start Export**. This will create a `.sql` file, which will be our backup.

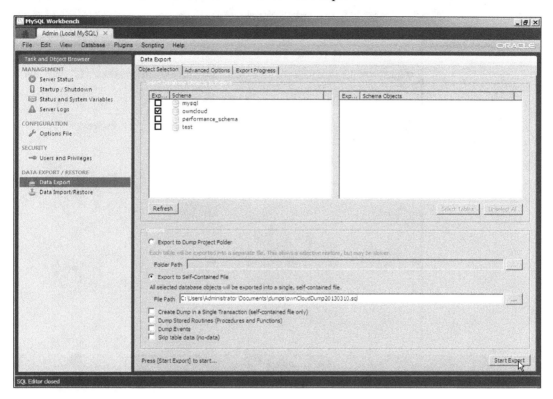

Once we click on the **Start Export**, the exporting process will begin, and a window confirming the same will show up. The `.sql` file, which is created, is nothing but a set of SQL commands to create the same database again. Please note that MySQL Workbench does not support scheduling out of the box.

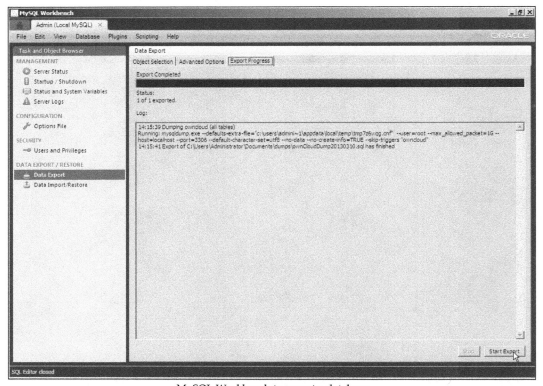

MySQL Workbench to export a database

Restoring is the process of getting the application back in working state. In case of ownCloud, we may want to restore after a system crash or we may want to move to a bigger machine. We will have to restore from a backup in such scenarios. Just like backups, restoring requires us to restore three components to restore ownCloud fully:

- config restore
- data directory restore
- database restore

First of all, we need to fetch all the components from the remote location, or wherever we stored them. We would recommend using `scp` because of security reasons, but any other suitable mechanisms can be used. Once we have these components with us, we can move ahead with the restore step by step:

1. Extract ownCloud downloaded from `ownCloud.org` to the document root of the web server or virtual host.
2. Now replace the config file from the backup with the config file already placed there.
3. Open the replaced config file, and check out the path of the data directory, and create it if it does not already exist.
4. Move the data directory from the backup to the data directory we just created.
5. Restore the database.
6. Done!

We can restore the database either by command line or by using MySQL workbench GUI. Let's walk through both the methods.

Because the `mysqldump` backup created before is nothing but a set to `sqlstatements`, which creates the exact replica of older database, we just have to make `mysql` execute all these SQL statements.

```
mysql -h localhost -u root -p <database_dump.sql
```

This functionality can be used to restore from a remote location by adjusting the −h parameter, which stands for a hostname.

Alternatively, we can use MySQL Workbench for the restore. We need to open the Workbench like before, and choose the appropriate server. In case the server is not there, we can add the same by clicking on the **New Server Instance**. In our case, since we are restoring from the same instance, we will choose the **Local MySQL**, and then click on **Manage Import / Export**. A prompt for password may appear. We can give the password here and click on the **OK** button.

On next screen we will choose **Data Import/Restore** from the left sidebar. Now we will click on the **Import from Self-Contained File** radio button, and provide it with the path of the `.sql` file we created during the backup process. After this, we will just click on the **Start Import**, and the database will be imported from the backup file.

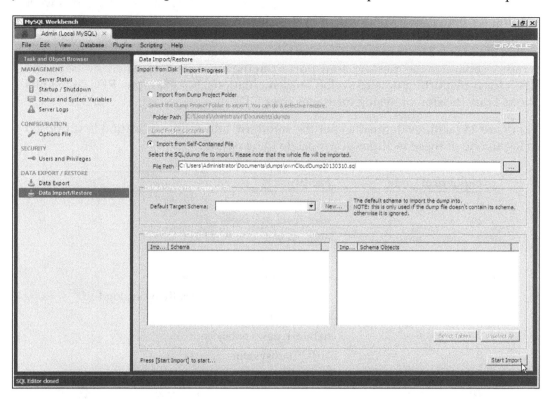

ownCloud logs

Logs are absolutely essential when things go wrong. Whenever we are trying to debug an application or we are just checking for failed login attempts or analyzing usage patterns, logs play a vital role. Talking about ownCloud, the two most important logs to analyze here would be the Apache logs, located in `/var/log/` directory and the ownCloud app logs itself, which are stored in data directory. For a single server deployment, we can just use `tail` or `less` to check out the logs easily, and see what is going on, but if the deployment is multinode or multiserver, then at times, correlating logs may become an issue. For such cases, we need to aggregate and merge logs at a single place, and syslog is just the perfect protocol to do that.

What is Syslog?

Syslog commonly refers to a data logging facility. Technically, it is a standard, not software, proposed by **Internet Engineering Task Force (IETF)** under RFC 5424 (`http://tools.ietf.org/html/rfc5424`). It is a relatively small RFC, and is worth reading for better understanding of Syslog. In any case, we will talk a bit about the standard and the RFC here. The standard is aimed to ensure interoperability of syslog standard. The standard does not talk about the backend storage of the data, it rather separates the message transport from the message data. There are separate RFCs for transporting data to syslog implementations. For example, RFC 5426 talks about Transmission of Syslog messages over UDP.

There are 24 facilities defined as per the standard, and each application is supposed to log to one of these facilities appropriate to its nature.

Numerical Code	Facility
0	kernel messages
1	user-level messages
2	mail system
3	system daemons
4	security/authorization messages
5	messages generated internally by syslogd
6	line printer subsystem
7	network news subsystem
8	UUCP subsystem
9	clock daemon
10	security/authorization messages
11	ftp daemon
12	NTP subsystem
13	log audit
14	log alert
15	clock daemon
16	local use 0 (local0)
17	local use 1 (local1)
18	local use 2 (local2)
19	local use 3 (local3)
20	local use 4 (local4)

Numerical Code	Facility
21	local use 5 (local5)
22	local use 6 (local6)
23	local use 7 (local7)

There are also severity levels defined to help in log management.

Numerical Code	Severity
0	Emergency: system is unusable
1	Alert: action must be taken immediately
2	Critical: critical conditions
3	Error: error conditions
4	Warning: warning conditions
5	Notice: normal but significant condition
6	Informational: informational messages
7	Debug: debug-level messages

A well-defined and structured syslog message will help in faster debugging and emergency response. Although developers may be interested in seeing Debug and Informational level messages to fix bugs, under normal circumstances, system engineers may be interested only in Warning and more severe issues.

Now that we have a basic knowledge of syslog standard, let's configure one of the implementations named rsyslog. Please note that rsyslog is different from syslog-ng, which is another syslog implementation.

Configuring syslog

Syslog can be used for collecting, processing, and storing the logs. There are two major alternatives when it comes to syslog, syslog-ng and rsyslog. Saying that one is better than other is a matter of personal preference and the requirement at the hand. Several Linux distributions use syslog-ng as their default syslog, but several others go for rsyslog. We are going to talk about rsyslog for now. The concept is similar for syslog-ng, just the syntax might vary a bit.

Let us configure rsyslog server for Centos 6. First, we need to install rsyslog, and using yum is the easiest way to do that.

```
$ yum install -y rsyslog
```

Now, we will choose a suitable transport protocol. We can either go with TCP or UDP. Although TCP will ensure the delivery of the message, it can have issues, if there are too many tcp messages in the queue. Depending upon the implementation of the rsyslog client the application may show degraded performance, because of TCP congestion control. If the rsyslog server and the ownCloud machine are in the same network or on the same machine, UDP probably would be a great choice. Let's see how to configure rsyslog to expose UDP listening port for receiving messages.

Find the following lines in /etc/rsyslog.conf, and uncomment them:

```
# Provides UDP syslog reception
#$ModLoadimudp
#$UDPServerRun 514
```

In case we wish to use TCP, we need to find the similar lines for TCP, and uncomment them:

```
# Provides TCP syslog reception
#$ModLoadimtcp
#$InputTCPServerRun 514
```

Also, let's aggregate all the messages coming to local1 facility to a file. We will send the Apache logs to this facility. Append the following to /etc/rsyslog.conf.

```
local1.*                        /var/log/apache.syslog.log
```

After this, we need to restart the rsyslog server, and we the can then see that rsyslog would be listening on port 514. This can be verified by using netstat utility.

```
# service rsyslogd restart
# netstat -anl | grep 514
tcp     0     0 0.0.0.0:514          0.0.0.0:*          LISTEN
udp     0     0 0.0.0.0:514          0.0.0.0:*
```

Now, let's configure the client side rsyslog, but this is to be done only if the Apache running ownCloud is on a different machine than rsyslog server. We wish to send the data logged to the local1 facility via UDP to the rsyslog server.

```
local1.*                        @syslog.browserstack.com:514
```

For tcp, just replace singe @ character by @@.

Now we need to configure Apache to log to the syslog facility instead of the default file. We can use ErrorLog directive for that. We just have to append the following to the ownCloud virtual host config and reload apache.

```
ErrorLog syslog:local1
# service httpd reload
```

With this, we are done sending Apache logs to rsyslog server. Now, let's send the ownCloud application logs to syslog. Fortunately, the ownCloud app comes with syslog support, so we don't have to do a lot to send the ownCloud app logs to syslog, but it does not support logging to a particular custom facility. So, for now, we will see that all the logs will go to either ` /var/log/syslog or /var/log/messages depending upon the operating system. To send the ownCloud application logs to syslog, open the config file and edit or append, if required, the following line in $CONFIG array:

```
'log_type' => 'syslog',
```

Once we are done here, the ownCloud application will start logging to the rsyslog's default facility.

These logs can be easily referenced later in case of need.

Summary

We discussed some of the many ways to create backups and do restores. We now know what it takes to create a full backup for ownCloud, and how to restore it when required. We also saw how logging can be handled for a big ownCloud installation. In all, we are now equipped with tools that can help us handle disasters better and perform an analysis to avoid them beforehand.

6
Load Balancing and HA for ownCloud

When we do large scale production deployments of ownCloud, we would want them to be always active and running. For corporates, universities, and service providers where any piece of infrastructure going down means loss of productivity and money, it becomes very important to ensure that ownCloud instance remains in a healthy state. In this chapter, we are going to discuss a few measures that can be taken by administrators to set up a highly available and fault-tolerant setup.

The key strategy

If we look closely for the purpose of load balancing, we will see three components in an ownCloud instance, which are as follows:

- A user data storage (till now we were using system hard disk)
- A web server, for example Apache or IIS
- A database, MySQL would be a good choice for demonstration

Now if we want to achieve high availability and load balancing for ownCloud, we have to do it for these components. There are a number of ways to achieve that and we are going to discuss some of them in context of ownCloud.

The user data storage

Whenever user creates any file or directory in ownCloud or uploads something, the data gets stored in the `data` directory. If we have to ensure that our ownCloud instance is capable to store the data then we have to make this redundant. Lucky for us, ownCloud supports a lot of other options out of the box, other than the local disk storage. We can use a Samba backend, an ftp backend, an OpenStack Swift backend, Amazon S3, Web DAV, and a lot more. We chose WebDAV as an example, because it illustrates the concept and it is fairly simple to implement without installing any more components.

Another thing we should always ensure that latency should be very low (around 10 ms) between the web server serving ownCloud and the external storage in order to have a good user experience, otherwise the whole ownCloud setup will appear to be lagging to the user.

Configuring WebDAV

Web Distributed Authoring and Versioning (WebDAV) is an extension of HTTP. It is described by the IETF in RFC 4918 at `http://tools.ietf.org/html/rfc4918`. It provides the functionality of editing and managing documents over the web. It essentially makes the web readable and writable.

We can configure WebDAV by using Apache modules. Let's see how it is done:

Apache's standard install already ships with the two required modules, which are `dav` and `dav_fs`. While the `dav` module allows creating, moving, copying, and deleting resources, `dav_fs` is its supporting module used to access the WebDAV server's filesystem. Let's include them in our Apache configuration by appending the following commands:

```
LoadModule dav_module modules/mod_dav.so

LoadModule dav_module modules/mod_dav_fs.so
```

It is a good idea, although not mandatory, to create a virtual host for WebDAV. So let us do it using the following code:

```
<VirtualHost *:80>
        ServerAdmin aditya@adityapatawari.com
    ServerName  webdav.owncloudbook.com
        DocumentRoot /var/www/webdav/root/
        Alias / /var/www/webdav/root/
    <Directory /var/www/webdav/>
            Options Indexes MultiViews
            AllowOverride None
```

```
                Order allow,deny
allow from all
</Directory>
<Location />
                DAV On
                AuthType Basic
                AuthName "webdav"
                AuthUserFile /var/www/webdav/passwd.dav
                Require valid-user
</Location>
</VirtualHost>
```

Now let's create the `Auth` file we just mentioned in the virtual host configuration. The `Auth` file is just a standard `htpasswd` file, which is given in the following command:

```
htpasswd -c /var/www/webdav/passwd.dav ocuser
```

That's it. Just reload the Apache server and we are good to go.

```
service httpd reload
```

It may be a good idea to check if the WebDAV server is actually working. We can do that by using a simple tool called `cadaver`, as given in the following command:

```
sudo yum install cadaver
```

```
cadaver http://webdav.owncloudbook.com
```

If we can see a prompt to the username and password fields, then our WebDAV is configured successfully.

Making ownCloud using WebDAV

To enable custom backend support, we will first have to go to the **Familiar Apps** section, and need to enable the **External Storage Support** app. After this app is enabled, when we open the ownCloud admin panel, we will see an external storage section on the page. Just choose WebDAV from the drop-down menu and fill in the credentials. Choose mount point as **0** and put the root as `$user/`. We are doing this so that for each user, a directory will be created on the WebDAV with their username and whenever users log in, they will be sent to this directory. Just to verify, check out the `config/mount.php` file for ownCloud. Our file will look as follows:

```
<?php return array (
    'user' => array (
      'all' => array (
```

```
       '/$user/files' => array (  'class' => 'OC_Filestorage_DAV',
'options' =>   array (   'host' => 'http://webdav.owncloudbook.com',
'user' => 'aditya',   'password' => 'mystrongpassword',   'root' =>
'$user/',   'secure' => 'false', ),),
       ),
    ),
);
?>
```

That's it! We have successfully configured ownCloud to use WebDAV.

The web server

Assuming that we have taken care of backend storage, let's now handle the frontend web server. A very obvious way is to do the DNS level load balancing by round robin or geographical distribution. In round-robin DNS scheme the resolution of a name returns a list IP addresses instead of a single IP. These IP addresses may be returned in the round-robin fashion, which means that every time the IP addresses will be permuted in the list. This helps in distribution of the traffic since usually the first IP is used. Another way to give out the list is to match the IP address of the client to the closest IP in the list, and then make that the first IP in the response of the DNS query. The biggest advantage of DNS-based load distribution is that it is application agnostic. It does not care if the request is for an Apache server running PHP or an IIS server running ASP. It just rotates the IP, and the server is responsible to handle the request appropriately.

So far, it sounds all good but then why don't we use it all the time? Is it sufficient to balance the entire load? Well, this strategy is great for load distribution, but what will happen in case one of the servers fails? We will run into a major problem then, because usually DNS servers do not do health checks. So in case one if our servers fail, we have to either fix it very fast, which is not easy always or we have to remove that IP from the DNS, but then the DNS answers are cached by several intermediate caching (only DNS servers). They will continue to serve the stale IPs and our clients will continue visiting bad server.

Another way is to move the IP from the bad server to the good server. So now this good server will have two IP addresses. That means that it has to handle twice the load, since DNS will keep on sending traffic after permuting the IPs in round-robin fashion.

Due to these and several other problems with DNS level load balancing, we generally either avoid using it or use it along with other load-balancing mechanisms.

Load balancing Apache is quite easy using Windows GUI

For the sake of this example, let's assume that we have ownCloud served by two Apache web servers at 192.168.10.10 and 192.168.10.11. Starting with Apache 2.1, a module known as `mod_proxy_balancer` was introduced. For CentOS, the default apache package ships this module with itself, so installing is not a problem. If we have Apache running from the yum repo, then we already have this module with us. Now, `mod_proxy_balancer` supports three algorithms for load distribution, which are as follows:

Request Counting

With this algorithm, incoming requests are distributed among backend workers in such a way that each backend gets a proportional number of requests defined in the configuration by the `loadfactor` variable. For example, consider this Apache config snippet:

```
<Proxy balancer://ownCloud>
BalancerMember http://192.168.10.11/ loadfactor=1 # Balancer member 1
BalancerMember http://192.168.10.10/ loadfactor=3 # Balancer member 2
ProxySet lbmethod=byrequests
</Proxy>
```

In this example, one request out of every four will be sent to `192.168.10.11`, and three will be sent to `192.168.10.10`. This might be an appropriate configuration for a site with two servers, one of which is more powerful than the other.

Weighted Traffic Counting

The Weighted Traffic Counting algorithm is similar to Request Counting algorithm with a minor difference, that is, Weighted Traffic Counting considers the number of bytes instead of number of requests. In the following configuration example, the number of bytes processed by `192.168.10.10` will be three times that of `192.168.10.11`:

```
<Proxy balancer://ownCloud>
BalancerMember http://192.168.10.11/ loadfactor=1 # Balancer member 1
BalancerMember http://192.168.10.10/ loadfactor=3 # Balancer member 2
ProxySet lbmethod=bytraffic
</Proxy>
```

Pending Request Counting

The Pending Request Counting algorithm is the latest and the most sophisticated algorithm provided by Apache for load balancing. It is available from Apache 2.2.10 onward.

In this algorithm, the scheduler keeps track of the number of requests that are assigned to each backend worker at any given time. Each new incoming request will be sent to the backend that has a least number of pending requests. In other words, to the backend worker that is relatively least loaded. This helps in keeping the request queues even among the backend workers, and each request generally goes to the worker that can process it the fastest.

If two workers are equally light-loaded, the scheduler uses the Request Counting algorithm to break the tie, which is as follows:

```
<Proxy balancer://ownCloud>
BalancerMember http://192.168.10.11/ # Balancer member 1
BalancerMember http://192.168.10.10/ # Balancer member 2
ProxySet lbmethod=bybusyness
</Proxy>
```

Enable the Balancer Manager

Sometimes, we may need to change our load balancing configuration, but that may not be easy to do without affecting the running servers. For such situations, the Balancer Manager module provides a web interface to change the status of backend workers on the fly. We can use Balancer Manager to put a worker in offline mode or change its loadfactor, but we must have mod_status installed in order to use Balance Manager. A sample config, which should be defined in /etc/httpd/httpd. conf, might look similar to the following code:

```
<Location /balancer-manager>
SetHandler balancer-manager

Order Deny,Allow
Deny from all
Allow from .owncloudbook.com
</Location>
```

Once we add directives similar to the preceding ones to httpd.conf, and then restart Apache, we can open the Balancer Manager by pointing a browser at http://owncloudbook.com/balancer-manager.

Load balancing IIS

Load balancing IIS quite easily uses Windows GUI. Windows Server editions come with a set of nifty tools for this known as **Network Load Balancer (NLB)**. It balances the load by distributing incoming requests among a cluster of servers. Each server in a cluster emits a heartbeat, a kind of "I am operational" message. NLB ensures that no request goes to a server which is not sending this heartbeat, thereby ensuring that all that the requests are processed by operational servers.

Let's now configure the NLB by performing the following steps:

1. We need to turn it on first. We can do so by following the given steps:

    1. Go to **Server Manager**.
    2. Click on the **Features** section in the left-side bar.
    3. Then click on the **Add Features**.
    4. Select **Network Load Balancing** from the list.

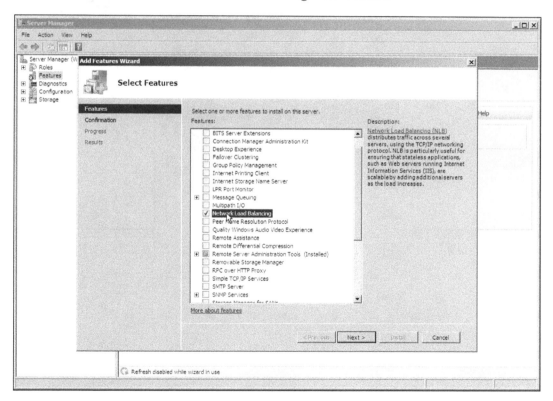

2. Once we have chosen **Network Load Balancing**, we will click on **Next >**, and then click on the **Install** to get this feature on the servers. Once we are done here, we will open **Network Load Balancing Manager** from the **Administrative Tools** section in the **Start** menu. In the manager window, we need to right-click on the **Network Load Balancing Clusters** option to create a new cluster, as shown in the following screenshot:

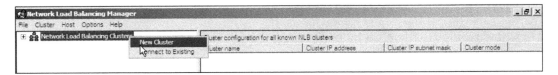

3. Now we need to give the address of the server which is actually running the web server, and then connect to it, as shown in the following screenshot:

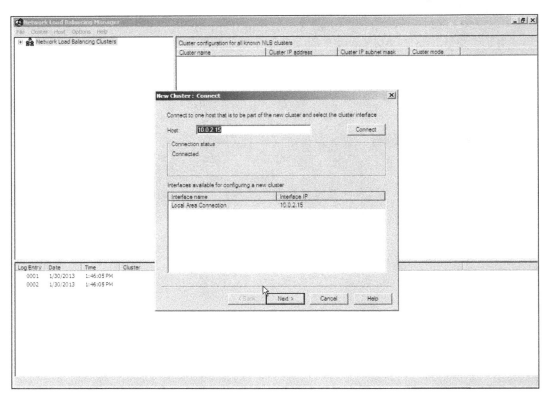

4. Choose the appropriate interface. In this example, we have only one, and then click on the **Next >** button. On the next window, we will be shown host parameters, where we have to assign a priority to this host, as shown in the following screenshot:

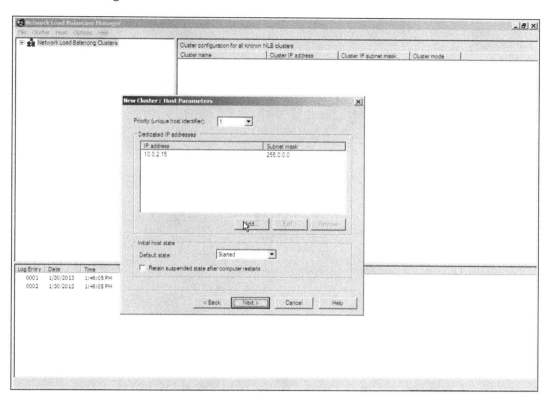

5. Now click on the **Add** button, and a dialogue will open where we have to assign an IP, which will be shared by all the hosts, as shown in the following screenshot. (Network Load Balancing Manager will configure this IP on all the machines.)

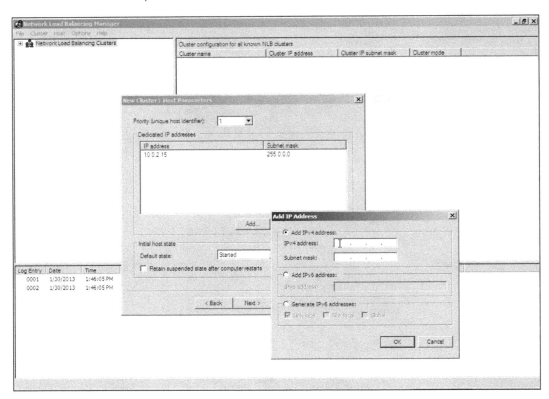

6. On the next dialogue choose a cluster IP, as shown in the following screenshot. This will be the IP, which will be used by the users to log in to the ownCloud.

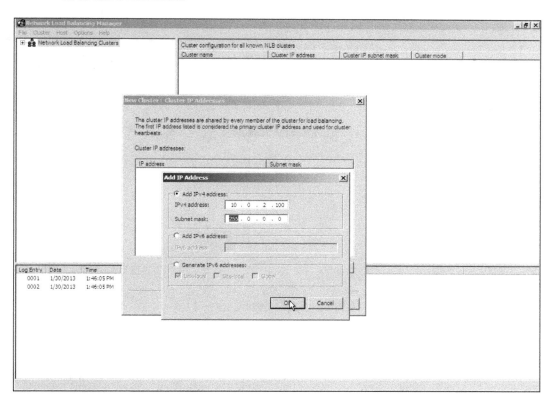

7. Now that we have given it an IP, we will define cluster parameters to use unicast. Multicasts and broadcasts can be used, but they are not supported by all vendors and require more effort.

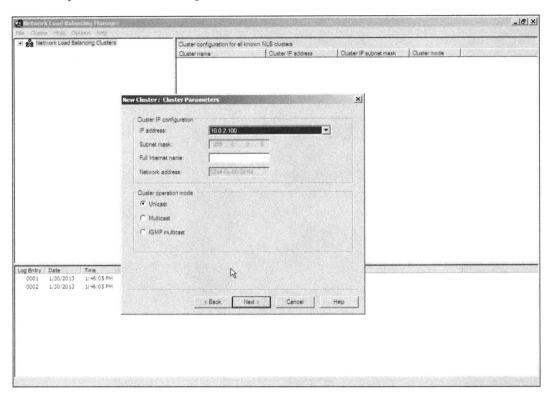

Now everything is done. We are ready to use the Network Load Balancing feature.

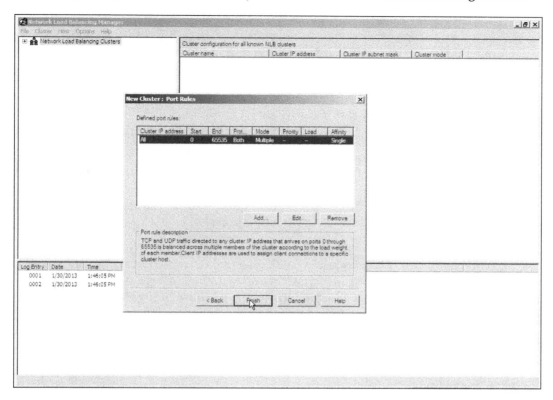

These steps are to be repeated on all the machines which are going to be a part of this cluster.

So there! We have also loaded balanced IIS.

The MySQL database

MySQL Cluster is a separate component of MySQL, which is not shipped with the standard MySQL server but can be downloaded freely from `http://dev.mysql.com/downloads/cluster/`. MySQL Cluster helps in better scalability and ensuring high uptime. It is write scalable and ACID compliant, and doesn't have a single disadvantage because of the way it is designed with multi masters and high distribution of data. This is perfect for our requirements, so let's start with its installation.

Basic terminologies

- **Management node**: This node performs the basic management functions. It starts and stops other nodes and performs backup. It is always a good idea to start this node before starting anything else in the cluster.

- **Data node**: This node will store the cluster data. They should always be more than one to provide redundancy.

- **SQL node**: This node accesses the cluster data. It uses the NDBCLUSTER storage engine.

The default MySQL server does not ship with the NDBCLUSTER storage engine and other required features. So it is mandatory to download a server binary, which can support MySQL Cluster feature. We have to download the appropriate source for MySQL Cluster from http://dev.mysql.com/downloads/cluster/, if Linux is the host OS or the binary if Windows is in consideration.

For the purpose of this demonstration, we will assume one Management node, one SQL node, and two Data nodes. We will also make a note that node is a logical word here. It need not be a physical machine. In fact, they can reside on the same machine as separate processes, but then the whole purpose of high availability will be defeated.

Let's start by installing the MySQL cluster nodes.

Data node

Setting up Data node is fairly simple. Just copy the ndbd and ndbmtd binaries from the bin directory of the archive to /usr/loca/bin/ and make them executable as follows:

```
cp bin/ndbd /usr/local/bin/ndbd
cp bin/ndbmtd /usr/local/bin/ndbmtd
chmod +x bin/ndbd /usr/local/bin/ndbd
chmod +x bin/ndbmtd /usr/local/bin/ndbmtd
```

Management node

Management node needs only two binaries, ndb_mgmd and ndb_mgm

```
cp bin/ndb_mgm* /usr/local/bin
chmod +x /usr/local/bin/ndb_mgm*
```

SQL node

First of all, we need to create a user for MySQL as follows:

```
useradd mysql
```

Now extract the `tar.gz archive` file downloaded before. Conventionally, MySQL documentation uses `/usr/local/` directory to unpack the archive, but it can be done anywhere. We'll follow MySQL conventions here and also create a symbolic link to ease the access and better manageability as follows:

```
tar -C /usr/local -xzvf mysql-cluster-gpl-7.2.12-linux2.6.tar.gz

ln -s /usr/local/mysql-cluster-gpl-7.2.12-linux2.6-i686 /usr/local/mysql
```

We need to set write permissions for MySQL user, which we created before, as follows:

```
chown -R root /usr/local/mysql

chown -R mysql /usr/local/mysql/data

chgrp -R mysql /usr/local/mysql
```

The preceding commands will ensure that the permission to start and stop the MySQL instance's remains with the `root` user, but MySQL user can write data to the `data` directory.

Now, change the directory to the `scripts` directory and create the system databases as follows:

```
scripts/mysql_install_db --user=mysql
```

Configuring the Data node and SQL node

We can configure the Data node and SQL node as follows:

```
vim /etc/my.cnf
[mysqld]
# Options for mysqld process:
ndbcluster                          # run NDB storage engine

[mysql_cluster]
# Options for MySQL Cluster processes:
ndb-connectstring=192.168.20.10  # location of management server
```

Configuring the Management node

We can configure the Management node as follows:

```
vim /var/lib/mysql-cluster/config.ini
[ndbd default]
# Options affecting ndbd processes on all data nodes:
NoOfReplicas=2    # Number of replicas
DataMemory=200M   # How much memory to allocate for data storage
IndexMemory=50M   # How much memory to allocate for index storage
                  # For DataMemory and IndexMemory, we have used the
                  # default values. Since the "world" database takes up
                  # only about 500KB, this should be more than enough for
                  # this example Cluster setup.

[tcp default]
# TCP/IP options:
portnumber=2202

[ndb_mgmd]
# Management process options:
hostname=192.168.20.10          # Hostname or IP address of MGM node
datadir=/var/lib/mysql-cluster  # Directory for MGM node log files

[ndbd]
# Options for data node "A":
                                # (one [ndbd] section per data node)
hostname=192.168.20.12          # Hostname or IP address
datadir=/usr/local/mysql/data   # Directory for this data node's data
files

[ndbd]
# Options for data node "B":
hostname=192.168.0.40           # Hostname or IP address
datadir=/usr/local/mysql/data   # Directory for this data node's data
files

[mysqld]
# SQL node options:
hostname=192.168.20.11          # Hostname or IP address
```

Summary

Now we have gained an idea about how to ensure high availability of ownCloud server components. We have seen the load balancing for backend data store as well as frontend web server, and the database. We have seen some common ways and we can now provide a reliable ownCloud service to our users.

7
ownCloud Application Development

ownCloud is awesome in itself. With the introduction of ownCloud apps, the whole thing goes to another level altogether. There are about a hundred apps hosted at `http://apps.owncloud.com/` easily dowloadable and ready to use. The effort which ownCloud community has put in is unparallel, but we are always looking for more and more contributors. So now we will see how to create an app and submit it to the ownCloud apps website at `http://apps.owncloud.com/`.

An ownCloud app is essentially a PHP pluggable module sort of thing, which we can just drop into a directory and it will start working. It has to have a defined structure so that it can integrate with ownCloud well. An ownCloud app can additionally have CSS and Java Scripts, following certain conventions, of course. Now let us check out these rules and conventions.

ownCloud app directory structure

Usually, ownCloud apps have files structured in the following directories:

- `ajax`
- `appinfo`
- `css`
- `img`
- `js`
- `l10n`
- `lib`
- `templates`

Not all the application will have all the directories. For a very small application, we may not need the `lib` directory or we may not need the `img` directory if our app doesn't have any image at all. Let us take a brief overview of each directory as follows:

- `ajax`: If our app has PHP scripts that answers AJAX requests then this is the directory in which we should place the scripts. This directory is not mandatory but is recommended to ensure that root of the app is clean and readable.

- `appinfo`: This is perhaps the most important directory of the application. It identifies the app and has the basic code required for its functioning. We also define information such as license under which the app has been released, version of the app, author information, and so on in this directory.

- `css`, `img`, and `js`: As the name suggests CSS files go in the `css` directory, images goes in the `img` directory, and JavaScript files go in the `js` directory. Although these directories are not mandatory, but if present they shouldn't be renamed.

- `l10n`: This directory contains translations. ownCloud looks for this directory and if it's ID is found, it immediately knows that the app can be translated. This directory is not mandatory.

- `lib`: If we end up writing a library for our app, then this is where the file will go. This helps in reducing noise in app's main code.

- `templates`: If the app uses templates, maybe to generate certain kind of generic pages, then those templates go into the `templates` directory.

Now that we are familiar with the structure and have got some idea about what it should look like, let us start going deeper into creating an app. ownCloud developer community helps us in this regard by providing app templates to play with. We will first set up the development environment, and then start modifying the code to suit our needs.

Setting up development environment

To set up our development environment, we need to obtain the code of ownCloud from github.com. Now ownCloud's code is divided into several components and together these components join to give us ownCloud. To obtain these components we will need git to clone a few repositories from github. Git is an open source version control system freely available at http://git-scm.com/download/ for all the major platforms. Linux users can use yum or apt to install git as well. Once we have git installed on our computer, we need to clone the code repositories. We will clone three repositories for now, which are as follows:

- core
- 3rdparty
- apps

As their names suggest, core consists of the core code of ownCloud. 3rdparty contains several third-party libraries, which are required for certain functionalities of ownCloud to work properly. The apps repository contains certain ownCloud apps. This repository also contains the application template in which we are interested. So let's clone these repositories one by one in the document root of web server as follows:

```
$ git clone https://github.com/owncloud/core.git owncloud
$ git clone https://github.com/owncloud/3rdparty.git 3rdparty
$ git clone https://github.com/owncloud/apps.git apps
```

Make the Apache server's user the owner of the directory and restart the Apache as follows:

```
$ chown -R apache owncloud
$ chown -R apache 3rdparty
$ chown -R apache apps
$ sudo service httpd restart
```

Use the ownCloud wizard to set up ownCloud using any web browser, similar to what we did previously.

Once the ownCloud installation is done, let's get a copy of the template to start modifying it as follows:

```
$ cp -r apptemplateadvanced myapp
```

Now we have our environment ready and we are going to start building our own awesome ownCloud app.

First, we need to put our new app into the `ownCloud` directory. We can either move it there or just create a soft link as follows:

```
$ sudo ln -s /var/www/apps/yourappname /var/www/owncloud/apps/myapp
```

According to ownCloud documentation we should change the following files and sections:

- AGPL headers for every file to reflect the author's name and other details.
- The `OCA\AppTemplateAdvanced` namespace to the `OCA\MyApp` namespace in every file.
- `dependencyinjection/dicontainer.php`: `parent::__construct('apptemplateadvanced')` to `parent::__construct('myapp')`
- `appinfo/info.xml` (personal settings)
- `appinfo/app.php` (the correct navigation settings)
- `appinfo/routes.php` (the name of the routes)
- `coffee/app.coffee` (the route names)

As we have already mentioned that for any app, the `appinfo` directory is the most important one, we'll start with editing certain parameters there. So let's start with the `info.xml` file in the `appinfo` directory. The XML tags defined there should be changed to reflect the app, which we are building as follows:

```
<?xml version="1.0"?>
<info>
<id>myapp</id>
<name>My App</name>
<description>The awesome app that I am building</description>
<version>1.0</version>
<licence>AGPL</licence>
<author>Aditya Patawari</author>
<require>5</require>
</info>
```

Although we defined a few parameters, there is another optional parameter which we didn't define here, and that is `types`; it defines the characteristics of the application, but many times if the application doesn't fall into any of the following defined types, then we can choose to ignore this property.

- **Prelogin**: These are the apps which are loaded before the user logs in to the account
- **Filesystem**: These are apps which provide functionality to interact with filesystems (for example, samba)

- **Authentication**: These are the apps which provide authentication backends (for example, the ldap application)

- **Logging**: These are the apps which are related to or define logging systems (for example, syslog)

Now let us modify app.php. As we have mentioned before, this is the file where we define the code for the app. As the bare minimum requirement, we need to modify the app.php file. Although the file is well commented, but still we would like to point out that ID is usually the app name and order is like weight of the app in the side navigation bar.

The href section points to the index of the app generally. Remember that this is a PHP app, and we get all the flexibility to do whatever we want. We can have the href pointing to my_non_conventional_file.php as well, but that would just make the code really bad and unconventional.

Although what we discussed was really enough for a bare-bones app, but we think a few more concepts need to be discussed before we see the code of an actual app. Let's us start by discussing Routes. Routes are nothing but a way to specify URLs. Now in the PHP world, file paths are URLs, but a lot more code is required if we want to do URL-based execution of code (for example if the values are to be extracted from a URL or a new instance of an application is to be created on receiving certain parameter in the URL). ownCloud uses Symphony routing (http://symfony.com/doc/2.0/book/routing.html). Symphony routing helps in creating clean, flexible, and SEO friendly routes easily. For ownCloud, routes are defined in appinfo/routes.php. It follows the following syntax:

```
// this route matches /index.php/yourapp/myurl/SOMEVALUE
$this->create('myapp', '/myurl/{key}')->action(
    );
```

Controllers are scripts which help in connecting templates with databases. Applications that do not need database access need not incorporate it. They must have a suitable entry in Routes for them to be callable. In general, a controller should be created following the general scheme of /controller/method/params.

For example, /mycontroller/mymethod/methods_param will signify a controller file named mycontroller.php in which we will define a function mymethod, which will take methods_param as an argument.

Database access for apps

AppTemplateAdvanced has a file in the appinfo directory for database access. The database.xml file is as follows:

```xml
<?xml version="1.0" encoding="ISO-8859-1" ?>
<database>
  <name>*dbname*</name>
  <create>true</create>
  <overwrite>false</overwrite>
  <charset>utf8</charset>
  <table>
    <name>*dbprefix*apptemplateadvanced_items</name>
    <declaration>
      <field>
        <name>id</name>
        <type>integer</type>
        <default>0</default>
        <notnull>true</notnull>
        <autoincrement>1</autoincrement>
        <length>4</length>
      </field>
      <field>
        <name>user</name>
        <type>text</type>
        <notnull>true</notnull>
        <length>64</length>
      </field>
      <field>
        <name>name</name>
        <type>text</type>
        <notnull>true</notnull>
        <length>100</length>
      </field>
      <field>
        <name>path</name>
        <type>clob</type>
        <notnull>true</notnull>
      </field>
    </declaration>
  </table>
</database>
```

Now the *dbname* and *dbprefix* needs to be changed depending upon the application usage. We can add a table by defining the `<table>` tag and add a field by defining the `<field>` tag. This is adopted from MDB2 XML schema notation. Note that ownCloud itself uses MDB2, but if PDO is present on the server, it will use that. Both of them help in database access.

Submitting an application to apps. ownCloud.com

Once we create an awesome app and we are ready to share it, we can upload it to `apps.owncloud.com` without any fee. We need to register there first and get our user ID. Once we have done this, we can just go to the **Apps** link on the top navigation bar and choose apps, and then add the chosen app. This will present us with a dropdown where we have to choose the category of the app, and then click on **Next**. A form will appear next, where we can give some screenshots, code, and other things. Once we save it, the app will appear at `apps.ownCloud.com`. Simple, wasn't it?

Inspecting a pre-built application

Let's walk through a simple pre-built app from the ownCloud app store to understand the applications better. We think the Notes app by *Robin Appelman* and *George Ruinelli* would be a good choice for this. Source for this app can be viewed on github at `https://github.com/owncloud/apps/tree/master/notes/`.

Now if we see the app we'll see that it has an `index.php` file. Although convention suggests that it should not be here, but this is the flexibility we get with PHP and ownCloud. Upon reading the file, we'll observe several references to `\OCP\`. To understand this, we need to understand the concept of ownCloud Classloader. Classloader is a functionality provided by ownCloud, due to which all the classes are loaded in the app automatically, with the exception of the third-party libraries. But we should keep in mind that to leverage this feature, our app's code should be organized as per the directory structure defined by ownCloud. The `index.php` file of notes app checks for various things such as is the user logged in or not, and if the app in enabled or not. It also loads Java Scripts and CSS files here.

Next up, we will have a look at the `appinfo` directory to verify what we just learned before. In the `appinfo` directory, we will see `app.php` and `info.xml` having the same pattern as we described before. It is worth noting that in `app.php`, the `href` attribute points to the `index.php` file we saw before.

The `ajax` directory has calls to retrieve and save notes, and `templates` directory holds a template to provide a way to create a new note and to provide a listing of other existing notes.

As obvious by the names CSS is in the `css` directory, JavaScripts are in the `js` directory, and localization files are in the `l10n` directory. The `lib` directory contains external third-party requirements (for example, markdown syntax). This is pretty much in line with what we have discussed before.

With this walk through we hope that we have helped in understanding ownCloud apps a bit better.

Summary

So we got started with building an application with ownCloud. We understood the directory structure, their routing mechanisms, and the Classloader. We also saw how a real app looks like. This chapter may appear a bit difficult if a clear knowledge of PHP is not there. By no means is this chapter exhaustive, and a full documentation for creating ownCloud apps can be found at `http://doc.owncloud.org/server/5.0/developer_manual/`. This chapter was just about how to get started.

Index

Symbols

UrlScan
  about 59
  URL 59
UrlScan.dll 59
UrlScan.ini 59
useradd command 58
user data storage
  about 86
  WebDAV, configuring 86, 87
  WebDAV usage, by owncloud 87
users
  creating 31

V

videos
  watching 28

W

WebDAV 86
Web Distributed Authoring and Versioning.
  See **WebDAV**
web server
  about 57, 88
  Apache hardening 57, 58
  hardening 57
  IIS hardening 59
  load balancing Apache 89
  Load balancing IIS 91-97
Web Server role 64
Weighted Traffic Counting algorithm 89
Windows Server 2008
  Active Directory, setting up 40-53

Thank you for buying
Getting Started with ownCloud

About Packt Publishing

Packt, pronounced 'packed', published its first book "*Mastering phpMyAdmin for Effective MySQL Management*" in April 2004 and subsequently continued to specialize in publishing highly focused books on specific technologies and solutions.

Our books and publications share the experiences of your fellow IT professionals in adapting and customizing today's systems, applications, and frameworks. Our solution based books give you the knowledge and power to customize the software and technologies you're using to get the job done. Packt books are more specific and less general than the IT books you have seen in the past. Our unique business model allows us to bring you more focused information, giving you more of what you need to know, and less of what you don't.

Packt is a modern, yet unique publishing company, which focuses on producing quality, cutting-edge books for communities of developers, administrators, and newbies alike. For more information, please visit our website: www.packtpub.com.

About Packt Open Source

In 2010, Packt launched two new brands, Packt Open Source and Packt Enterprise, in order to continue its focus on specialization. This book is part of the Packt Open Source brand, home to books published on software built around Open Source licences, and offering information to anybody from advanced developers to budding web designers. The Open Source brand also runs Packt's Open Source Royalty Scheme, by which Packt gives a royalty to each Open Source project about whose software a book is sold.

Writing for Packt

We welcome all inquiries from people who are interested in authoring. Book proposals should be sent to author@packtpub.com. If your book idea is still at an early stage and you would like to discuss it first before writing a formal book proposal, contact us; one of our commissioning editors will get in touch with you.

We're not just looking for published authors; if you have strong technical skills but no writing experience, our experienced editors can help you develop a writing career, or simply get some additional reward for your expertise.

OpenStack Cloud Computing Cookbook

ISBN: 978-1-84951-732-4   Paperback: 318 pages

Over 100 recipes to successfully set up and manage your OpenStack cloud environments with complete coverage of Nova, Swift, Keystone, Glance, and Horizon

1. Learn how to install and configure all the core components of OpenStack to run an environment that can be managed and operated just like AWS or Rackspace

2. Master the complete private cloud stack from scaling out compute resources to managing swift services for highly redundant, highly available storage

Apache CloudStack Cloud Computing

ISBN: 978-1-78216-010-6   Paperback: 294 pages

Leverage the power of CloudStack and learn to extend the CloudStack environment

1. Install, deploy, and manage a cloud service using CloudStack

2. Step-by-step instructions on setting up and running the leading open source cloud platform CloudStack

3. Set up an IaaS cloud environment using CloudStack

Please check **www.PacktPub.com** for information on our titles

Instant VMware vCloud Starter

ISBN: 978-1-84968-996-0   Paperback: 76 pages

A practical, hands-on guide to get started with VMware vCloud

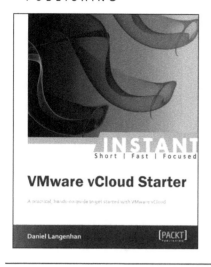

1. Learn something new in an Instant! A short, fast, focused guide delivering immediate results

2. Deploy and operate a VMware vCloud in your own demo kit

3. Understand the basics about the cloud in general and why there is such a hype

4. Build and use templates to quickly deploy complete environments

IBM Websphere Portal 8: Web Experience Factory and the Cloud

ISBN: 978-1-84968-404-0   Paperback: 474 pages

Build a comprehensive web portal for your company with a complete coverage of all the project lifecycle stages

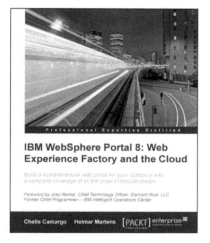

1. The only book that explains the various phases in a complete portal project life cycle

2. Full of illustrations, diagrams, and tips with clear step-by-step instructions and real time examples

3. Take a deep dive into Portal architectural analysis, design and deployment

Please check **www.PacktPub.com** for information on our titles

www.ingramcontent.com/pod-product-compliance
Lightning Source LLC
Chambersburg PA
CBHW060151060326
40690CB00018B/4073